Developing Basketball Intelligence

Tactical Skills and Game Awareness for the Advanced Player.

By Brian McCormick

ISBN: 978-0-557-04335-4

1. Sports – Basketball. 2. Coaching. 3. Physical Education and Training – Basketball.
I. McCormick, Brian, 1976 –

Brian McCormick

highfivehoopschool@yahoo.com

Published by Lulu

Printed and bound in the United States of America

Cover design: John Hayashi / Inkblot Creative Asylum / inkblot.ca@gmail.com

Thank you to my advisors on this project:

Rick Allison, Brianna Finch, and Derek Vargas

Other books published by Brian McCormick:

Cross Over: The New Model of Youth Basketball Development

Blitz Basketball: A Strategic Method for Youth Player Development

Championship Basketball Plays

180 Shooter

Hard2Guard: Skill Development for Perimeter Players

Hard2Guard Player Development Newsletters, Volume 1

Hard2Guard Player Development Newsletters, Volume 2

Paperback books available at www.lulu.com/brianmccormick.

E-books available at www.180shooter.com.

Table of Contents

For information on Camps and Clinics, visit:

www.developyourbballiq.com

Introduction

Developing Basketball Intelligence introduces basketball intelligence as a trainable skill and provides a template for coaches to use to develop their players' basketball intelligence. Basketball intelligence combines tactical understanding with game awareness and decision-making skills. It is the capacity to make the right decision given a certain situation and to execute the play. An intelligent player exhibits the qualities of an expert performer. He:

- Reads the game and understands what is happening;
- Anticipates how the play is likely to develop based on processing the given information;
- Draws on past experiences when confronting a given situation and makes the correct decision;
- Executes quickly with an appropriate skill level (Wein).

Characteristics of an Intelligent Player

- Chooses the best option in less time
- Looks for the best solution by prioritizing alternatives, calculates the risk inherent to each and maintains focus until he makes the right decision
- Knows the right play to make at any moment of the game relative to the time and score
- Never rushes and always feels secure and confident when making a move
- Uses his eyes to see the entire court and always appears to have time to make a play
- Balances taking risks and making the easy play
- Adapts to ever-changing situations
- Knows when and where to pass and when it is better to attack with the dribble
- Possesses good spatial awareness – correctly assesses the distance between he and a teammate or defender
- Keeps the game simple
- Knows what he is going to do with the ball before he receives it
- Uses his creativity for the team's benefit
- Knows how to play the game, especially away from the ball

The "Sports Cognition Framework" describes three elements needed for sports success:

1. Decision-Making Ability: knowing what to do
2. Motor Skill Competence: being physically able to do it
3. Positive Mental State: being motivated and confident to do it (Peterson)

Developing Basketball Intelligence focuses on the first element, the decision-making skills. To execute the skills, players need the ability and the confidence and motivation; the following outline contributes to the development of technical skills, confidence and motivation. However, the primary focus is the elusive decision-making skills which often separate the elite performers from the average players. This does not dismiss the importance of ability, confidence or motivation, as the three elements work together in sports performance.

Basketball is a fast-paced game which requires players to make split-second decisions. Players who anticipate and make decisions faster than their opponents have a decided advantage, and those players who make quicker and more accurate decisions exhibit basketball intelligence. These players "exhibit superior anticipatory performance compared with less skilled performers…skilled players made a decision approximately 140ms earlier than less skilled players did, thereby providing a considerable performance advantage," (Williams, et. al).

Basketball tends to be a traditionalist sport; we believe players are born with court vision and a high basketball I.Q., so we ignore its development. Coaches and players at the highest levels believe in its innate quality and these beliefs filter through the development system, which emphasizes recruiting the talented player rather than developing these skills in the players on the current roster. "I don't know where it comes from but either a player has it or a player doesn't have it," NBA Hall of Fame inductee Rick Barry said. "I can teach you how to pass but I can't teach you how to see. If I throw you a pass into that little hole in the defense – that to me is the one telling thing that determines whether you're a natural player," (Farrey).

These skills can be taught. Players can improve their anticipatory performance, "presumably as a result of a more refined ability to pick up subtle cues and to ignore irrelevant sources of information," (Williams, et. al). To develop basketball intelligence, we must develop players' perceptual skills so they know what to read, when to read it and how to respond to what they read. Therefore, we need to change our approach to skill development, as the traditional block practice, technical approach fails to enhance game intelligence. Developing Basketball Intelligence outlines a different approach based on a global coaching methodology, a tactical approach (as opposed to a technical approach) and a *Teaching Games for Understanding* model.

In its purest sense, a global coaching methodology is playing the game; on the other end of the spectrum is an analytical methodology in which the coach uses very precise instructions (Kidman). With an analytical methodology, the coach tells the player exactly where to place his foot, when to move his foot and where to go: he sets up a drill where the offensive player starts at the three-point line, makes a jab step and a crossover step move to the basket. The coach corrects each move until it is perfect, with the player stepping exactly six inches on his jab step, sweeping the ball below his knees and driving past an imaginary defender on his crossover step. In a global methodology, the coach sets up a 1v1 scenario and tells the offensive player to score. The perfect methodology exists somewhere along the spectrum and depends on the skill level and experience of the players. However, a global coaching methodology helps players to develop the decision-making skills necessary to play successfully in a game.

An analytical methodology uses a technical approach to skill development. Teams practice and develop individual technical skills (shooting, passing, dribbling) and leave players to discover how to link these skills in a dynamic game environment (Villepreux). A technical approach depends heavily on a coach's strategy as the team relies on set plays to produce good shots.

A global methodology uses a tactical approach to skill development. Rather than practice the individual skills in isolation, players develop their technical and tactical skills simultaneously by playing the game or modified games (Villepreux). Players use their tactical skill understanding to produce good shots.

A player's success in a game situation depends on his ability to read the defense, quickly make the appropriate decision and execute the play in the dynamic environment. There are no "fixed" conditions during a game. When the player learns the jab-and-crossover-step move in an isolated drill with constant coach feedback, he does not adjust to the defender's presence. In the game, with a defender present, the defender creates a new skill. The player cannot pre-determine the jab-and-crossover-step move; instead, he must adjust to the defender and the defender's reaction to the jab step. "The ability to quickly and efficiently vary a previously learned skill is only possible when the player has been exposed to a systematic development of his intellectual capacity," (Wein). The global methodology and tactical approach provide the systematic development of a player's intellectual capacity because a coach's feedback centers on the appropriateness of the decision, rather than the preciseness of the step. The player learns the skill against a defensive player, rather than in isolation, so he is prepared for the defender in the game.

The <u>Teaching Games for Understanding</u> model builds on the ideas of the global coaching methodology and the tactical approach. The TGfU model includes six steps (Butler and McCahan):

1. *Game*. Modify the rules, equipment, playing area and group size so every player plays.
2. *Game appreciation*. Players learn and respect the rules.
3. *Tactical Awareness*. Players understand the game by solving problems in game situations.
4. *Decision making*. Players practice elements of decision making, which include:
   - Selective attention: paying attention to relevant cues
   - Anticipation: anticipating opponent's response
   - Using the appropriate skill
5. *Skill execution*. The game play motivates players to learn skills and the skill development enhances the play performance.
6. *Performance*. Players improve as this cycle continues.

For young or novice players, we modify the game to introduce the basic skills and rules in a fun environment where they have room to use and develop their skills. Younger players need more practice with lots of room, while advanced players need to practice in tighter spaces (Launder). In a technical approach, when a coach aims to lighten practice or add a fun drill, he uses a relay race or similar competition. However, relay races do not teach game skills. How often does a player dribble in one straight line from baseline to baseline?

Instead, a TGfU model uses a modified game, like *2v2 Rugby*, to create a competitive learning environment where players practice a speed dribble and open court lay-ups, but use the basic game rules and learn the general game flow and strategy: the game is not just a race, but the offense competes to score, while the defense attempts to stop the offense and gain possession of the ball so it can score. Introducing young or novice players to a game like *2v2 Rugby* rather than relay races introduces the players to the game form, generates game appreciation, introduces basic tactical awareness (force jump shots not lay-ups, pass to the open player), begins to develop decision-making skills (pass or dribble; stop the ball or protect the basket) and trains the same technical skills used in relay races (dribbling, passing, shooting lay-ups).

As players gain more experience, the cycle continues, as players develop more advanced skills through the game play and the games involve more players. Rather than practicing different finishes around the basket based on the coach's instructions, the player uses the appropriate finish based on the defense. The coach adds complexity to the exercises based on the players' ability, experience and performance. The coach creates an initial situation through the game form and rules – in *2v2 Rugby*, the offense cannot pass the ball forward in the back court to encourage trapping by the defense. Players solve the problem (the trap) and based on the coach's perception of their performance, he adds increased difficulty or eases the restrictions (Villepreux).

Developing basketball intelligence is more time consuming and a more difficult process than teaching players several set plays, a well-organized press break and a basic defensive scheme. However, everyone wants players with basketball intelligence: players who always seem to be in the right spot and make the right play. Typically, the players who possess the advanced decision-making skills and anticipation skills which characterize an intelligent player are the players who progress to the next level.

Some great coaches use the analytical, technical approach. They micromanage their players and do not attempt to develop their basketball intelligence. They run set play after set play and discourage players from thinking. If these coaches succeed at the highest levels, why should youth coaches spend time and energy developing basketball intelligence rather than skipping to technique development and performance?

Many coaches criticize today's players because they "do not know how to play the game." Shortly after taking over as Head Coach of the Charlotte Bobcats, Larry Brown said:

> "The things they don't know boggle my mind…Like when you're on the weak side on defense and you have to see man and ball. Like talking on defense. Like denying one pass away. Or, if a guy drives baseline on you, how you have to fold back and take the big guy of the board. Like throwing it to the first open man instead of faking to that guy. There's a reason he's open, right?" (McCallum)

Players lack this game intelligence because coaches feel the pressure to win or perform right away, so they do not feel they have the time to develop their players' basketball intelligence, as it is a lengthy process. Coaches focus on the quickest path to improvement rather than long term development. "This rigid and authoritarian coaching style doesn't develop intelligent players with awareness and responsibility," (Wein). If a player never plays for a coach who takes the time to teach these skills, provides feedback based on the player's decision-making and puts the player into game situations in training where he can make and learn from mistakes, how is he supposed to develop this game intelligence? When coaches use the technical skill development approach, players are on their own to develop the game awareness and decision-making skills which ultimately determine their success.

Approaching a team with the intent to develop basketball intelligence forces a coach to use a different strategy than a coach who settles for memorization and set plays. The coach must insure that his players learn and take responsibility for their learning and their actions. He must accept mistakes as part of the learning process and encourage questions. He must use questions as part of his teaching strategy to guide the players' learning. He must focus beyond the result and concentrate on the process. In short, a coach who decides to develop basketball intelligence commits to an empowerment coaching style using an athlete-centered philosophy and a long term approach, the three basic tenets of Cross Over: The New Model of Youth Basketball Development.

When players have more freedom, and they know that the coach trusts them, players learn more and have more fun. They enjoy the problem solving aspect of different situations on the court because they have the mental skills to choose the right play.

John Wooden developed "players who were creative, confident problem solvers. He taught that it is the opponents that determine a team's responses during a game. He wanted us to be so automatic in our basketball fundamentals and so versed in the concepts that we were ready to quickly devise our own solution methods for the constantly changing problems our opponents posed," (Nater and Gallimore). Basically, he wanted basketball players, and he sought to develop basketball intelligence.

Chris Paul possesses basketball intelligence. We characterize players as possessing a "high basketball I.Q." frequently, but what do we mean by this description? It means the game "slows down" for Paul, and he "sees" the play before it occurs. We use these expressions commonly, and we accept the notion that one player plays the game in slow motion while everyone moves at regular speed and that some players see into the future. Maybe we should incorporate psychic training in young players so they too can see into the future and possess this mystical quality!

Instead, these often used and rarely explained phrases have meaning which is relevant to skill development. "Expert performers are not endowed with superior visual function...perceptual and cognitive factors are better discriminators of skilled performance in adults...Experts typically exhibit more effective search strategies...and are faster and more accurate at recognizing and recalling patterns of play from memory," (Ward and Williams). When faced with a situation, a player with basketball intelligence recognizes and recalls the situation faster and more accurately than an average player which leads to faster and better decisions. In a game where every split-second matters, making faster decisions plays a big role in a player's success.

We have two dimensions to our attention: internal-external and broad-narrow (Nideffer). When our attention is internal, we attend to our own thoughts; when it is external, we attend to our environment through our senses. When we have a broad attention, we see things through a wide lens; with a narrow attention, we zoom on specific details. With two dimensions, we can characterize our attention in four ways: broad-external, broad-internal, narrow-external and narrow-internal.

Everyone has a limit to the amount of information he can process at one time. Think of your brain as a camera that takes 40 pictures per second (Nideffer). In normal situations, your brain takes an equal number of pictures in each concentration area. However, if you shift your attention, you can take more pictures in the desired area. When we say that the game "slows down" for Chris Paul, we mean that Paul directs his attention appropriately; he shuts off his own thoughts, so he takes 40 external pictures. Therefore, he sees more. He sees important postural cues that other players miss simply because he concentrates appropriately at the right time.

Beyond using the correct attentional style at the correct time, Paul ignores unimportant information and focuses on the most relevant information or cues. When penetrating with the basketball, he takes in the entire court; however, with his attention directed appropriately, he sees things that average players miss. When he sees these visual cues, like a defender shifting his weight or changing his stance, he combines them with his advanced search strategies based on his experience which helps him to anticipate the play. Because he anticipates, he "sees the play before it occurs."

As Paul dribbles in the key, he notices Tyson Chandler's defender slightly turn his shoulders toward the ball and he sees Peja Stojakovic's defender playing him closely at the three-point line. Paul knows that Chandler's defender loses vision of Chandler when he turns his shoulders. He also knows that Chandler runs to the rim whenever the defender gives him the opportunity. As soon as Paul sees Chandler's defender turn his shoulders toward the ball, he knows that Chandler will cut and his defender will be a step late based on the accumulation of experience with the defender's position, so he leads Chandler to the basket with a well-paced pass. At game speed, the pass and dunk appear magical, almost unfair. Paul is just too good. He was born with eyes in the back of his head. Instead, his mental processes create the play at a subconscious level without Paul devoting any conscious effort to thinking about which pass to make. Paul noticed the defender move and reacted immediately with the pass.

We think that we see superior vision from an innately talented superstar. In reality, we see the results of basketball intelligence. Paul perceives and interprets information in a more efficient and more effective manner, and his perceptual-cognitive advantage develops through specific adaptations that occur through extended engagement in the sport," (Williams and North).

If these skills develop through sports engagement, they are as much environmental as they are innate. Therefore, how can we develop these qualities in all young players? First, we must understand the skills that we hope to develop and the best way to develop those skills.

Basketball is an "open skill sport" – each action depends on the actions of teammates and opponents. However, we spend a disproportionate amount of time working on closed skills and technique where the coach predetermines the skill execution. Closed skill practice does not transfer to games because of the

> **Closed Skills** occur under fixed conditions, are predictable and have clearly defined beginning and ending points, like a free throw.
>
> **Open Skills** occur in a changing environment where decisions and adjustments must be made "on the run," like leading a fast break.

game's random nature. In practice, the player executes the skill, but in the game the defense changes the skill. The drill fails to develop the full skill; instead, it trains the technique. It ignores the perceptual and decision-making skills which are highly influential in determining success (Dick). Therefore, our first change is to develop open skills.

With a global coaching methodology, a coach "introduces the ball according to which game situation he wants to simulate," (Kidman). Rather than break practice into chunks or blocks, where players practice one skill (shooting) and then move to another

> **Technique**: the closed-skill mechanics.
>
> **Skill**: the open-skill execution of a technique with its perceptual, decision-making and contextual elements.

(team defense), the coach organizes a modified game to train the skill or concept that he wants to practice. He sets up the modified game and allows the players to play through the situation. For instance, rather than practice a 5v0 press break until players memorize the precise cuts, he plays a 4v5 game and instructs the five-man team to trap all over the court as if they were down five points with 30 seconds to play. The offensive players adjust and adapt to the situation and learn how to move the ball. The coach presents a problem (playing a man down and facing full court pressure), and the players devise a solution. If the players struggle, the coach stops the action and uses a practice block to teach the proper spacing or the best way to cut against pressure. However, players direct the learning through their play, and the coach uses questions to enhance the learning.

On a simplistic level, the Teaching Games for Understanding model uses a Game-Practice-Game model or the whole-part-whole teaching method. This does not mean that the coach "rolls out the ball and lets them play." This approach requires a strong pedagogical approach. The coach uses the games to dictate the practice within a training session. Wayne Smith, Head Coach for the All Blacks, New Zealand's National Rugby Team, says: "I don't have a book of drills because every time I go out there, I do something new. Drills develop from the last training and reflect what we are trying to achieve next week," (Kidman). Coaches observe the performance and teach based on their observations, adding or subtracting complexity when necessary.

The traditional approach to sport practice is behavioral training, which uses block training. To practice a pick-and-roll, the team spends 10 minutes running a pick-and-roll drill with the ball handler using the pick and attacking the basket, and then using the pick and passing to the screener rolling to the basket. Players practice going shoulder to shoulder on the screen and the screener practices opening to the ball when he rolls. They practice the technique of setting and using a screen, and the coach insures perfect execution before moving to the next block. Optimal learning occurs if the players perform one repetition every seven seconds (Peppler).

Block training leads to immediate improvement in practice performance. However, the immediate gains do not equal learning, as learning requires relatively permanent changes in performance and retention from

> **Block Training** = Short-term Memory
> **Random Training** = Long-term Memory

one session to the next (Schmidt). Skill gains in practice might be the result of temporary factors. In a subsequent session or game, the temporary effects dissipate, leaving a lower performance level than during practice (Schmidt). Block training stores the information in short-term memory (Peppler), which is why your players forget how to use the screen at practice tomorrow.

Because players do the same thing over and over, their practice performance improves. However, they do not necessarily learn the skill. Schmidt uses this example:

> You are in 5th grade, and you want to learn to do long division "in your head." In deliberate blocked practice I ask you, "What's 36 divided by 12?" You struggle, finally coming to the answer "3." On the next trial, I ask you, "What's 36 divided by 12?" Your performance is facilitated now because you remember the answer you just gave, so you don't have to generate the answer again.

> If I gave you 10 of these in a row, your performance would be perfect (or nearly so), but you would not be exercising the generation of the solution, only the repetition of the remembered answer. This is an example where a factor that facilitates performance in practice (blocked repetitions of a particular division problem) is detrimental (as compared to a randomized presentation of several problems) to learning and measured on tomorrow's test (Schmidt).

If the players do the pick-and-roll drill over and over, they improve at the drill. The guard remembers to go shoulder to shoulder, and the post remembers to open to the ball. The guard delivers the pass at the right moment, and the post makes the lay-up in perfect stride. We end the block session feeling as though we made progress and the players understand the pick and roll. We have a false sense of confidence because we believe that we developed the skill because our practice performance improved. However, in the next game, when the defense traps the pick and roll, the guard picks up his dribble as he is ill-equipped to handle the new situation even though the coach devoted a large part of practice to the pick and roll. The performance improvements during the block practice do not transfer to the game.

Instead, the new approach to skill development is random or variable practice (Vickers). Random training uses game play to develop skills. Rather than the coach controlling the learning, the players control the learning through their play. Rather than a scripted drill, the players play. Learning can only be measured by changes in performance (Schmidt) and random training goes into your long term memory (Peppler).

Random training is not all good. When players have control, the play can get ragged and sloppy. This necessitates practice. After watching the team play, and observing their performance, the coach uses an appropriate drill to teach a missing concept or develop a skill. If playing a modified game emphasizing the pick-and-roll, the coach may use the practice portion to walk-through the proper spacing or teach the ball handler to use a fan dribble to create space if the defense traps or teach the screener the proper way to roll. If the ball handler just faced five straight traps, and did not make the correct play, he is ready to learn so he can improve his performance. The random training dictates the block training and puts the work into long-term memory (Peppler).

During the block practice session, the coach creates cues which he can use in the game play. One cue, for instance, is a base set. In a Triangle offense, the base is a strong side triangle with two players on the weak side. When the players get sloppy, and the spacing breaks down, the coach cues the players by saying "Base!" or "Triangle!" to remind the players of the basic positioning. The players know the base set and quickly move to regain their shape. This is a reaction or response cue, as the coach responds to a mistake (Peppler).

To develop the proper responses before a mistake, use *lead cues*: cue the proper response *before* the need for the behavior (Peppler). When the coach sees the trap developing, he cues the ball handler with "space, space," or he cues the screener with "slip." The coach helps the players with their recognition. The cues must be succinct, and the player must have the ability to respond. The players make the right play because you lead them to the proper behaviors and responses rather than responding to mistakes (Peppler). The random training anchors the block training cues, so players store the learning from the block training in their long term memory and anticipate the play the next time they face the same situation.

The lead cues teach the players what to look for while it is happening rather than teaching based on the player's memory or through video. When the screener hears the coach yell "Slip!" and feels his defender losing contact too early, he learns the proper cue for the future. In the game, when his defender loses contact too early, he slips to the basket because he learned the appropriate response, and it is stored in his long term memory.

Meaningful improvement requires deliberate practice: the coach provides timely and meaningful feedback; players have a specific goal; and players get numerous repetitions. To develop the pick-and-roll, the coach sets up the activity with a specific goal – for instance, 2v2 half court with the offense using a pick-and-roll before scoring. Players get far more repetitions in various skills in a 2v2 or 3v3 game than when playing 5v5. The coach offers intermittent feedback, combining questions and cue words to facilitate the players' development. On a turnover, the coach asks the passer "What caused the turnover?" which forces the passer to think about his mistake and ultimately learn from the mistake. If the defense hedges too early, the coach yells, "Slip! Slip!" to cue the screener. The coach also could stop the action to revise the technique: some coaches yell "Freeze!" so players stop in their tracks and the coach can rewind the play or illustrate the problem based on the current positioning. If the coach wants to practice a complimentary skill, like splitting the trap with the dribble, he stops the game and sets up a drill where players use a hesitation and a low, long dribble to split through stationary defenders (chairs). After several repetitions to teach players the right technical approach, the players return to the small-sided games to use the new technique against live defenders.

Small-sided games are an ideal learning environment because they provide plentiful repetitions like block training with the variables of random training. "For skills learning…the secret is to condition/modify games to the extent that the movement required occurs more often, but do so under varying conditions…the sooner a practice can be put into more realistic game-like situations, the better," (Kidman). The movement in 3v3 is similar to 5v5. Running a pick-and-roll in a 3v3 game is the same as running a pick-and-roll in a 5v5 game. The difference is the spacing of the non-involved players and their help defenders. However, the skill execution and initial reads are the same.

In the coaching process, the coach must use lead cues selectively as a teaching tool, and not as a crutch to make decisions for players. Behavioral training typically uses constant feedback, while random training uses reduced feedback (Vickers). Beyond cues, use questions to help the players develop their basketball intelligence. Players remember better when they discover the answers for themselves, rather than a coach giving them the answers. "The solution they generate is theirs and thus athletes will take ownership and remember, understand and apply the content more effectively than if they were told what to do, when to do it and how to do it," (Kidman).

Initial skill improvement is often better with behavioral training, but athletes do not maintain or improve these performances long term (Vickers). Random training takes more time because coaches teach players to think for themselves. To develop more intelligent players, coaches need to stimulate more and instruct less (Wein). "The acquisition of experiences and knowledge is much better when it is a result of a well-proven pedagogical process where the coach uses questions and demonstrations to unlock the development of experiences and knowledge so that they are clearly understood," (Wein).

More than simple technique development, a coach must ensure that a player develops the skills to play in a game; otherwise, players train for the sake of training. Practice sessions build to competitive play, and the practice sessions have value if the lessons transfer during competition. Therefore, "develop games that insure that skills occur and develop in context…Emphasize shifting to perception (reading the game) and decision making, based on players having the knowledge and gaining responsibility for training and performance," (Kidman).

Through the focus on open skills and variable practice, players develop better game awareness, and skills transfer from practice to game situations. Players learn to read situations and anticipate the next play. When coaches give players the opportunity to play, they have more meaningful experiences and think for themselves. The players direct their learning, and the coach enhances the learning through questions which force players to search for the right answers. Players become active learners, engaged in the skill development, rather than passive learners trying to absorb their coach's instructions. Each situation becomes a learning opportunity. As these learning opportunities add together, players' cognitive-perceptual skills become more refined and efficient, and they make more accurate and quicker decisions.

The subsequent chapters outline the games and drills to use to develop the basic tactical skills. Each section includes representative questions for the coach to use in his evaluations of the team's performance, and other questions to use with the players to enhance their development.

Recently, I went to a basketball academy and watched the young players dribble. I marveled at their technical ability. They could do every drill. However, when they scrimmaged, nobody ever used the dribble to go anywhere, and few players could beat their defender. The technical skill did not transition to the game because the players lacked the basic athletic skills (evading, agility) and tactical skills (decision-making and perceptual skills) to use the dribble as a weapon.

FULL COURT SITUATIONS

The full court section teaches players to attack an individual defender in open space and when tightly defended. This is game ball handling, rather than technique practice, focusing on the skill of using the dribble in a game. Most teams use 1v0 lay-up drills or a chair to teach open court moves. Game mistakes occur when a player uses the wrong technical skill, not because of poor technical execution: players misread the situation more often than they dribble off their foot (obviously, younger and less experienced players require more technique practice to prevent dribbling off their foot). Reading the defender and understanding one's strengths against the defender lead to success. Young players often assume that a defender's presence requires a change of direction move; however, oftentimes, a simple hesitation move beats a poorly positioned defender. Use this section to teach players how to beat a defensive player based on situational cues and use the games to train against a live defender.

Attacking a Defensive Player in Open Space

When an offensive player attacks a defender in open space – the offensive player is dribbling toward his offensive goal with a defender waiting in his path – the offensive player's greatest advantage is speed in the desired direction. The offensive player attacks forward, while the defender must slow the offensive player while moving backward to protect the basket. As the offensive player approaches the defender, the defender typically tries to influence the ball handler in one direction. As the ball handler approaches, he evaluates two cues:

1. Does the defender present a top foot or are his feet parallel?
2. Is the defender playing the ball (typically in the ball handler's outside hand) or the inside shoulder (if the ball is in the inside hand, the defender has to play the inside shoulder)?

If the defender's feet are parallel, no move is needed: pick your strong hand and attack directly past the defender. The defender has no chance to stop a speed dribble with his feet parallel if the offensive player attacks in a straight line rather than bellying out. Get low, protect the ball with your inside shoulder and drive directly past the defender, eliminating any angle of recovery.

If his feet are not parallel, attack his top foot: in the middle of the floor, most defenders influence to the offensive player's weak (left) hand, so the defender puts his left foot forward. As you approach the defender with a right-hand dribble, make an in-n-out move to move the defender toward your midline and then attack past the defender's left shoulder forcing the defender to turn his hips. With a left-hand dribble, make a low crossover move and attack to your right.

Another option is to attack based on his location. If you attack with speed, and the defender plays your inside shoulder, a speed dribble or a slight hesitation dribble is enough to create an angle to the basket. On the right side, if the defender plays toward the offensive player's left shoulder, attempting to keep him from the middle, a simple hesitation beats the defender. A straight line drive is always faster, and preferable, to a change of direction. Therefore, if the defender's right foot is his top foot, but he plays the inside shoulder, attack with the straight line drive rather than making the crossover move. In this case, he protects the middle, so his weakness is the straight line drive. If the defender plays the ball, then attack the lead shoulder (top foot). On the right side, if the defender's left foot is forward, use an in-n-out move to create a little space and attack with a straight line drive; if the right foot is forward, make a crossover move as you approach the defender.

In a 1v1 situation, these are the two most important cues: the defender's location in relation to the ball and his stance. An offensive player can influence these factors. For instance, if he is on the right side and wants to shoot a right-handed lay-up, he attacks with the left hand dribble. The defender will move to the inside shoulder, opening the outside lane to the basket: approach with a hard dribble toward the middle and then cross over to the outside and finish with the right hand lay-up. If offensive players learn to read these cues, their success will improve. Teach players the cues to read and they will have more success. Use the different variations of the *Foster's Drill* to practice reading the defense and finishing.

Drill: **Foster's 1v1 Drill**	
Objective	To read a defender's positioning in the open court and make the appropriate tactical decision while attacking full speed with the dribble.
Pre-requisites	Speed dribble with both hands; hesitation move; in-n-out move; crossover move; lay-up; power lay-up and crossover lay-up.
Drill Execution	Offensive player starts on the baseline and the defender starts at the free throw line with a ball. Defender passes to the offensive player, sprints to half court, turns and plays defense. Offensive player receives the pass and attacks the opposite basket. Offense gets one shot. Go to the end of the line and switch offense and defense on the next turn.
Progression I	Offensive player starts at half court and the defender starts at the top of the key. When the coach says, "Go!" the offensive player races to the opposite free throw line and the defender touches the baseline. The offensive player touches the opposite free throw line, turns and receives a pass from the coach. The defender touches the baseline and sprints forward. Offensive player attacks the basket; defender tries to prevent the offensive player from getting into the lane. Offense gets one shot.
Teaching Points	Straight-line drive is better than a change of direction; attack the defender with speed and put him on his heels; stay off the sideline – allow space to go around a defender to the sideline side; attack at 80% speed so you can accelerate past a defender if necessary; once you beat the defender, cut off his angle of retreat; and protect the ball on your shot – do not "rock the cradle."

If players struggle to get to the basket and finish, determine the reason.

- Do the players struggle with their technical skills, either the lay-ups or the open court moves?
- Do they make the wrong move at the wrong time?
- Do they lack confidence in their weak hand which leads to poor decisions?

If players struggle with their technical skills, break down the session into the "part" practice and work on the weakness. Build the skill gradually, loading the skill step by step from a point where the players are successful to a return to the live game moves.

If players make the wrong move, simplify the read. Rather than reading the defender's shoulder and location, teach them to read the defender's location and make a definitive move – speed is the great equalizer. A decisive move made quickly often works even if it is technically the wrong decision. Give players three options:

1. If the defender plays the outside hand, crossover;
2. If the defender plays the offensive player's midline, use an in-n-out move;
3. If the defender plays the inside shoulder, use a hesitation and go.

This is like lead cuing – you give the players the cues beforehand to enhance the players' performance. By starting with one decision, players learn to focus on the appropriate cues.

Attacking when Tightly Defended

Attacking a defender in the full court when tightly defended uses some of the same concepts as attacking a defender in the open court and is similar to attacking in live ball situations. There are two general situations that occur:

1. The offensive player receives a pass while defended and starts from a live ball position, like when receiving the inbounds pass against a man-to-man press.
2. The offensive player is defended closely after he has dribbled, like a defender picking up the offensive player who takes off with the dribble after a rebound.

The reads and decisions differ slightly based on the situation and the offensive player's goals. If the opponent's defense is retreating quickly, the offensive player's goal may be to advance the ball up court without a turnover and enter into the offense. However, the offensive player may think that if he can beat the initial defender quickly, he can create a transition situation for his team.

When the offensive player starts from the live ball, his goal is to beat the defender with his first two dribbles. Like with the above concepts, he should read two cues:

1. Lead shoulder
2. Location

He must be aware of his pivot foot when making his move. If the defender uses a staggered stance with a lead foot, he shows a lead shoulder. Rather than looking at the defender's feet, if the offensive player looks at his shoulders, he keeps his eyes up and sees the lead foot. Defenders try to influence players to their weak hand or to the sideline. Either way, between their location (inside shoulder or the ball) and their lead shoulder, they show a path of least resistance. Few defenders are smart enough to give the path of least resistance in the direction they desire, like toward a help defender's trap, because few players read the defense in this manner. Defenders think that they are forcing an offensive player in some direction, when they often are giving away a free lane.

If you catch the ball on the right side, and the defense forces you to your left hand, he is likely to give the entire left side. To "force" you left, he puts his left foot forward and plays your right shoulder; if he plays the middle of your body or the inside shoulder with the left foot forward, attack with the right hand and force the defender to switch his hips, giving you a two-step advantage. Assuming he plays the right shoulder, a good move with the left hand (direct drive or crossover drive depending on your pivot foot) leads to an almost straight line drive toward your basket. The defender loses a step and must catch up from behind.

Once the player dribbles, he has several questions to resolve:

1. Does the defender have an angle?
2. Are you attacking at an angle with a defender on your hip or are you attacking with a straight line drive with the defender sprinting to recover?
3. When he catches up, does he play the inside shoulder or the level of the ball (on a speed dribble, the level of the ball is always in front of the ball handler)?
4. How fast are you attacking? Do you have room to accelerate?
5. Are there any help defenders in the way or do you have a clear lane?
6. Is the goal to get the ball into the front court or to create a transition situation?

Using these questions teaches the player to read the cues and make appropriate decisions. If a mistake occurs, asking questions helps lead the player to the answer, which improves learning, retention and transfer. Use different full court 1v1 games to practice these skills.

Game: Full Court 1v1	
Objective	To develop confidence handling the ball under pressure.
Pre-requisites	Speed dribble; protect dribble; space dribble; crossover move; lay-up; power lay-up; and crossover lay-up.
Drill Execution	Offensive player starts on the baseline; defender checks the ball by putting the ball on the ground. The ball is live as soon as the offensive player picks up the ball. Offensive player attacks to the other basket; defender contains the dribble and attempts to force a turnover. Offense gets one shot to score. Pair goes to the end of the line and switches offense and defense on their next turn.
Progression I	Play to one basket. When the defensive player forces a turnover or gets a rebound, he attacks his basket. No out of bounds on loose balls. When finished, go to the end of the line and switch offense and defense next time.
Progression II	One player starts on each baseline. Coach tosses the ball. Whoever gets the loose ball plays offense and attacks the basket opposite of his starting position, while the other player plays defense. Play to one basket. When the defensive player forces a turnover or gets a defensive rebound, he attacks his basket. No out of bounds on loose balls. When finished, go to the end of your line.
Teaching Points	Use a change of pace dribble to control the defender; minimize playing with the ball; keep shoulders squared to the basket – no side to side dribbles; attack the defender's lead shoulder; cut off his angle of retreat; and protect the ball on your finish – do not "rock the cradle."

Assess the mistakes:

- Do the players need more technical practice?
- Do they read the cues correctly?

If they make mistakes, they may need more experience in the game/drill rather than moving to a more simplified version. However, if the mistake is something like a frequent traveling violation on the player's first step, practice the jab step, drive step and crossover step in a more controlled drill and gradually load the skill back to the full drill/game.

LIVE BALL SITUATIONS (HALF COURT)

In addition to ball handling, players need live ball moves or moves from the Hard2Guard position. Basketball is a team game requiring five players to work together for the team's benefit. However, within the team game are many 1v1 scenarios: attacking one defender after a steal, getting open to receive a pass, handling the ball against a man-to-man press, creating one's own shot and more. To play the team game successfully, individuals must win the individual battle.

Some coaches do not like players to make individual plays. However, as scouting becomes more prevalent, especially at the higher levels, individual plays are more and more important. When the defense is set and organized, the offense needs an individual play (dribble penetration, screen, skip pass, post entry) to disorganize the defense and give the offense an advantage.

Players are most open when they first receive the pass – either they receive the pass in open space, or their defender is moving toward them, giving them the opportunity to make a move against their defender's momentum. If the defense is out of position, either because they gave too much space or because they are out of control when closing out, the offensive player should make an individual move, whether shooting the open shot or driving the bad closeout. The following is a 1v1 progression to practice the moves, and more importantly, the reads for individual moves.

Catching in Open Space

When waiting for a pass on the weak side with your man playing help defense, evaluate your options to facilitate a quicker decision when the pass arrives. Anticipate the pass. If your defender moves toward the midline, a good pass means a shot: set your feet and be ready to shoot. A defender cannot close out from the middle of the key to the three-point line quick enough to defend a shot.

If the defender plays closer to you, read his movements and your teammate's movements. Be aware of your post player on the block – if you receive a quick ball reversal, your post player may establish deep post position, which might make a post entry pass the desired response.

Be aware of dribble penetration, traps and double teams. The following chapters cover spacing in detail, but prepare to move to an open spot or basket cut when the situation develops.

On the catch, if the defender is too close to shoot, read the direction and speed of his closeout:

1. Is his closeout in a straight line between you and the basket? Is he below the straight line or above the line?
2. Is he close enough to close out under control or is he sprinting?
3. Is he in position to change directions or is his weight too high or too forward to stop a drive?
4. Is he aware of your location or must he locate you first?
5. Can you move out of his peripheral vision to force him to pay attention to you (good for your teammates) or lose vision (good for you)?

If his closeout is below the line between you and the basket, the middle of the floor is open (Figure 1); if his closeout is above the line, the baseline drive is open (Figure 2). If he is out of control, a shot fake and a drive against his momentum may be the best play. If he has no vision, cut to the basket if the area is open or relocate to a new spot. Take advantage of his mistake or weakness. If he is too focused on the ball, punish him with a cut. If he is too quick to take away your shot, drive past his closeout; if he is too slow, punish him with the shot. However, start the decision-making process by anticipating the pass and evaluating the defender's position.

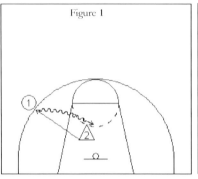

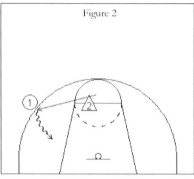

Drill: 1v1 Closeout

Objective	To read the defender's closeout and attack with a shot or move directly from the catch to use the defender's forward momentum against him.
Pre-Requisites	Catch-and-shoot shots; lay-ups; shot fake.
Drill Execution	Form a line on the left wing above the free throw line extended (P3). One player (P1) starts on the right wing as the offensive player and another player (P2) starts on the midline as the defender. The play starts when P3 throws a skip pass to P1; however, the ball is not live until P1 touches it. P2 closes out to play defense and the offense plays to score. Play until P1 scores or P2 gets a rebound or steal or the ball goes out of bounds. P3 moves to defense and the winner plays offense: if P2 stops the offense, he plays offense; if P1 scores, he remains on offense. The loser goes to the end of the line.
Variations	Play from different spots on the floor and different angles of closeout. Limit the number of dribbles.
Teaching Points	Know your strengths; make a decision while the ball is in the air – if you are a shooter, a good pass leads to a shot and you adjust on a bad pass; read the angle of the closeout; attack against the defender's momentum; follow your shot.

Catching when Tightly Defended

When receiving the pass when tightly defended, the shot is likely not the best option. Instead, feel the defender's pressure and make a move against his momentum. Otherwise, square to face the basket, read the defender while you square and make the best decision.

1. Is the defender off balance?
2. Is the defender favoring or influencing to a side?

3. Is the defender in position to take away the immediate attack?
4. Does the defender go for fakes or is he disciplined?

As you square, read the defender's lead shoulder and positioning. A good defender is tough to beat once he gets his feet set, as he positions himself to take away your best options, and the help defense positions itself to help on any penetration. Therefore, look to make the move on the catch, as you square to the basket, to take advantage of the defender's momentum.

Drill: 1v1 Check

Objective	Assess strengths and weaknesses, read the defense and take the first opening. Many players make a move (jab step for instance) and the defense reacts (jumps back), but the offensive player is not prepared to take advantage (shoot or attack with a crossover drive).
Pre-Requisites	Jab step; space step; the Box; drive step; and pivot foot.
Drill Execution	Form a line at the top of the key. First player starts on offense and next player starts on defense. The defender checks the ball by setting it on the ground, and the ball is live when the offensive player touches it. The defender plays defense, and the offense plays to score. Play until the offense scores or the defender gets a rebound or steal or the ball goes out of bounds. Next player in line enters on defense, and the winner plays offense: if the defender stops the offense, he plays offense; if the offense scores, he stays. Loser goes to the end of the line.
Variations	Play from different spots on the three-point line. Limit the number of dribbles.
Teaching Points	Attack the lead shoulder to force the defender to switch his hips; drive directly past the defender – do not "belly out" or make a "banana" drive; attack to the basket, not to the baseline; get low on your first step – try to get your shoulders even or past the defender's body; sweep the ball and pivot to protect the ball – do not turn your back and "turtle" with the ball.

Drill: 1v1 Wing Entry

Objective	To feel the defense on the catch and make a move immediately to go against his momentum: beat the player once (to get open), not twice.
Pre-Requisites	V-cut; L-cut; front pivot; reverse pivot; the Box; sweep moves.
Drill Execution	Form a line at the top of the key. One player starts on offense at the right block and another player starts on defense. Using only the right side of the court, the offensive player cuts to get open and the defender denies the pass. The offensive player has five seconds to get open; the ball is live once the passer passes. When the offensive player receives the pass, the defender plays defense and the offense plays to score. Play until the offense scores or the defender gets a rebound or steal or the ball goes out of bounds. Passer moves to defense, and the winner plays offense: if the defender stops the offense, he plays offense; if the offense scores, he remains on offense. The loser goes to the end of the line.
Variations	Change the starting spot, receiving spot and passing angle. Limit the dribbles.

Teaching Points	Step into the defender and then break away – no dancing; hook to the ball on the catch; sweep, pivot and make a move directly from the catch; attack the defender's forward momentum.

Review the mistakes and determine whether players need more experience with the games or if they need part practice to break down the skill. Review the Hard2Guard moves.

The Hard2Guard moves build from the basic concepts like the direct drive, crossover drive, front and reverse pivots and the sweep move. Once players learn the basics, they combine the different concepts into a series of moves based on the situation and reading the defense.

- **Direct drive**: drive in the direction of the lead (non-pivot foot) foot. The first step and the hand which dribbles are on the same side of the body.

- **Crossover drive**: the lead foot steps across the body to attack in the direction of the pivot foot. The first step and hand which dribbles are different.

- **Front Pivot**: the body turns in the direction it is facing; the pivot follows the toes.

- **Reverse Pivot**: the body turns away from the direction it is facing; the pivot follows the heels.

- **Sweep and Go**: Use a reverse pivot and sweep the ball low, below the knees. The reverse pivot is the first step in a direct drive to the basket. On the right side, the right foot is the pivot foot. The reverse pivot is a 180-degree pivot, and the left foot leads the direct drive to the left of the defender (the defender's right). The pivot and first step are one move. As the player steps with his left foot, he dribbles with his left hand and extends past the defensive player.

If the offensive player gets his shoulders even or past the defensive player, he cuts off the defender's angle of retreat. Take a big first step and keep "nose over toes." Attack the defensive player and be strong with the inside shoulder to protect the ball and the drive line. Extend with the dribble. On a crossover drive, sweep the ball low, outside the box, to move the ball from the right hand to the left hand to start the move. Combine the basic concepts to make the appropriate move based on the situation and the defense.

Passing instruction often focuses on the proper passing technique. The chest pass is the most over-taught skill because it is useless when a player is defended, yet it comprises the bulk of passing instruction in youth basketball. Players understand the idea of passing to a teammate – every team sport or game involves this concept. Passing technique is easy to master. Therefore, why are there so many passing mistakes and turnovers?

The defense changes everything about a pass, from its speed to its direction to the type of pass. In a passing drill, the player devotes his attention to the pass execution and his target. He has a narrow-internal focus on his personal execution of the passing technique and a narrow-external focus on his target. In a game, he needs a broad-external focus: at minimum, he must see his defender, his target and his target's defender. When his defender applies more pressure, the passer's attention narrows, as he concentrates more on protecting the ball than finding an open teammate, and his field of vision narrows: we call this "tunnel vision."

To promote effective passing, players need to be strong and confident with the ball so they can account for the three things: defender, target and the target's defender:

Defender

- How is my defender defending me?
- Is he quick?
- Where are his hands?
- Where are his eyes?
- Does he go for fakes?
- Do I have a dribble to use to create a passing lane?

Target

- Is he open?
- Is he standing still or on the move?
- Does he cut aggressively to the ball?
- Is he using a screen?
- Where is he cutting?
- Is he going to curl or flare?
- Where are his eyes?
- Does he feel his defender?
- Will he respond to me if I make a pass fake to get him to cut elsewhere (fake a pass to the wing to create a backdoor cut)?
- Will he finish his cut or will he break off the cut if the pass is not immediate?
- Is he cutting to get open or is it a cut to set up a cut (v-cut)?
- Are his hands up?

Target's Defender

- Where is he?
- Is he trailing or denying?

- Will he fight through the screen?
- Will the defense switch?
- Is he in position to steal a pass?
- Does his positioning dictate a certain pass (lob, bounce, etc)?
- Is he focused on the ball?
- Does he go for fakes?

Many times, the passer must answer these questions, and more, while dribbling the ball down court at full speed or when under pressure from a defensive player. Therefore, the more confidence that the player possesses in his ball skills, the more attention he can focus externally on his target. In a game, he does not process these questions one by one at a conscious level. Instead, in an instant, he sees his defender, his target and his target's defender, processes the information, makes a decision at a subconscious level and executes the skill. When you drive your car, you do not consciously ask yourself a series of questions moment by moment; however, based on experience, you are constantly judging the distance between you and the car in front of you and the likelihood that the light will turn red. If your kids in the backseat keep fighting with each other, you divert some of your attention to dealing with your kids, leaving less attention to focus on the cars, the road and the signals.

If the passer lacks confidence dribbling or possessing the ball under pressure, his attention will not be directed correctly – like the driver with the fighting kids – and he will throw the ball to a player before his teammate is ready or he will not see the trailing defender cutting in front for the steal or he will forget that his teammate flares off every screen. The pressure and/or lack of confidence leads to a rushed decision as the player's field of vision narrows as his attention shifts from finding the open man to protecting the ball from his defender.

In addition to the ball skills from Chapter 2, teach these five skills to build players' confidence with the ball when they face pressure defense or do not have the dribble:

- **The Box**: The area in the middle of the body between the chest and the top of the knees. When moving the ball from side to side against pressure, keep the ball out of the box and rip the ball across the player's hair line or under the player's knees.
- **Space Step**: A longer step used to create space to shoot or to relieve pressure. While protecting the basketball (Diamond the Ball) with the width of the body, step directly between the defender's legs, leading (but not swinging) with the hip and elbow. Then, reverse pivot to face the basket.
- **Diamond the Ball**: Protect the ball by the back ear, with elbows out, forming a diamond (right). The position prepares players to make a quick overhead pass, to pass fake or to go up for a put-back. Against pressure, Diamond the Ball and use a space step to create space and relieve pressure.

- **Pass Fake**: Used to move the defense or hold the help defense, similar to a quarterback faking a hand-off to hold the linebackers. Never pass in the direction of a pass fake. Use against the player covering the pass receiver or against a zone defense.
- **Ball Fake**: A small, quick fake used to create a passing angle. Use against the player defending the passer. Fake low

to make an air pass or fake high to throw a bounce pass. The pass follows directly from the fake with no wasted motion.

GETTING OPEN

Passing and receiving is a team skill. However, getting open to receive the pass is often a 1v1 battle. Most teams use screens to make it easier to get open, but players need the ability to get open without a screen. Getting open is a basic evading skill: set up the defender in one direction and cut in the other or use a change of pace to create separation.

Before teaching V-cuts and L-cuts and down screens, train players to evade defenders, create space and get open on their own. General tag games during warm-ups develop agility and evading skills. Next, begin with games and drills which incorporate passing and getting open in an unstructured environment. If players struggle, add some instruction (V-cuts) or structure to the drills.

Game: Volleyball Passing	
Objective	To pass and cut in tight spaces.
Pre-Requisites	Chest pass; bounce pass.
Drill Execution	Use the volleyball court lines between the 10-foot line and the end line as the boundaries and divide players into two four-man teams. Play a passing game to 100 completed passes with no dribble. On a turnover, the player who committed the turnover runs out of bounds and runs a lap around the court before re-entering the game (if a team has a sub, the player runs the lap, tags his teammate, and the sub enters the game). The score continues: teams pick up at their previous score when they committed a turnover.
Teaching Points	Pass and cut; spread the court; be strong with the ball; pivot and see the court.

Game: Full Court 3v3/No Dribble	
Objective	To pass under pressure and to create passing lanes with aggressive cuts.
Pre-Requisites	V-cut; L-cut; ball fake; pass fake; the box; diamond the ball; and lay-ups.
Drill Execution	Play 3v3 full court. No dribbling allowed. Play to three baskets. Any ball which goes out of bounds goes to the defense.
Teaching Points	Cut to get open; set screens to get open; flash hard to the ball; show a target to the passer; use ball fakes to create a passing lane.

Game: 2v2 Gael Passing	
Objective	To be strong with the ball under pressure, to create passing lanes and to work on the timing between passer and receiver.
Pre-requisites	V-cut; L-cut; ball fake; pass fake; the box; and diamond the ball.
Drill Execution	Play 2v2 within the three-point line. No dribbles allowed. Winner is the first team to complete seven consecutive passes. Start at zero on each change of possession. Play from the point of the turnover or steal: do not set up at the top every time. Any ball that goes out of bounds goes to the defense.

Variation	Play 2v2 within the three-point line. Each offensive player gets one dribble each time he catches a pass. Start at zero on each change of possession. Play from the point of the turnover or steal: do not set up at the top every time. Any ball that goes out of bounds goes to the defense.
Teaching Points	Use the entire area; cut against the defender's momentum; see your teammate; pivot to protect the ball; use eye contact to communicate; show a target; use a ball fake to get your defender's hands out of the passing lane; use the dribble judiciously; and be physical – step into the defender and cut away to create a passing lane.

Use the games to evaluate players' strengths and weaknesses. Observe their mistakes and use the questions to determine the practice block:

- Does the passer allow the pressure to force him into a bad pass?
- Does the passer's defender deflect the passes?
- Is the passer passing off his back foot?
- Does the target's defender steal the pass?
- Is it a soft pass or does the target wait for the ball?
- Does the receiver take a poor angle?

If the passer makes the mistake, review the five Hard2Guard skills and use the *1v1 Hard2Guard Drill* to review the skills and work on the basics of protecting the ball.

Drill: 1v1 Hard2Guard Drill

Objective	To be strong with the ball and maintain a positive stance rather than turtling.
Pre-Requisites	Hard2Guard position; Diamond the Ball; Space Step; The Box.
Drill Execution	Divide players into pairs around the three-point arc with one ball per pair. One player starts on offense with the ball and the other starts on defense. For 30 seconds, the defensive player attempts to steal the ball, while the offensive player protects the ball and stays squared to the basket. After 30 seconds, switch offense and defense.
Teaching Points	Keep the ball active; stay out of the *Box*; use the *Space Step* to drive the defender back; pivot to protect the ball; be strong with the ball.

If the receiver makes the mistake, teach V-cuts and L-cuts and use the following drills. When we start with instruction, players concentrate on the correct execution of the V-cut, not on getting open. Use the instruction to supplement their natural instincts, rather than stifle them, or to offer guidance for players who struggle to find open space on their own. For young players, finding space and moving to open areas is more important than how they get there.

More important than the technique of the cut is learning to run all the way to the catch when closely defended. Turnovers occur when the receiver waits for the pass, and the defender cuts in front. Use *Two-Man Pressure Passing Drill, Box Passing Drill* and *Gauntlet* to train receiving the pass under pressure and pivoting to see the court.

Drill: 2-man Pressure Passing

Objective	To be strong with the ball and make aggressive cuts all the way to the ball.
Pre-Requisites	V-cut; L-cut; ball fake; pass fake; the Box; Diamond the Ball; wrap-around pass; push pass.
Drill Execution	Divide players into two lines on the baseline, one along the sideline (L1) and one at the lane-line (L2). L1 starts with the ball; L2 sprints forward about 20-feet and then cuts back toward the ball. L1 passes to L2. L2 catches the pass with feet in the air, lands with a quick stop and pivots to face up court. L1 sprints 20-feet past L2 and cuts back to the ball. He receives the pass, quick stops and pivots. Work from one baseline to the other and return on the other half of the court.
Progression	Add defensive players. Offense sprints up court and breaks back to the ball to get open. Passer protects the ball using pivots and fakes and passes to his teammate when he is open. Start over from the point of the pass on a turnover.
Teaching Points	Be physical; get the defender's hand out of the passing lane; pass to your teammate's outside hand; create a passing lane; keep head and shoulders with the ball – use pivots, sweeps and fakes; keep the ball active.

Use the *2-man Pressure Passing Drill* to teach and train V-cuts and L-cuts. When trying to get open to receive a pass, offensive players often make one of three mistakes:

1. They dance with their defender.
2. They avoid contact.
3. They take a poor angle.

The *2-man Pressure Passing Drill* addresses each of these mistakes. Offensive players must be physical with the defense and get the defender's hand out of the passing lane. When tightly defended, offensive players must protect the pass first and then make a move: they must cut hard all the way to the ball. Pass receivers must make cuts: when players "dance" (shuffle back and forth two to three steps with the defender) they confuse the passer because the passer never knows when the cutter is making a cut. Make straight line cuts and meet the defender's physicality.

Drill: Box Passing

Objective	To get open and to pass under pressure.
Pre-Requisites	Chest pass; bounce pass; push pass; pivot foot.
Drill Execution	Divide players into two teams, an offense and a defense. The offense starts in a box formation with players at each elbow and each block and one player at the top of the key (O1), while the defenders guard each offensive player. O1 starts with the ball and calls the name of a teammate (O2); O2 must cut to get open for a pass anywhere on the court. O1 cannot dribble and the other players must remain stationary. After completing the pass to O2, O1 fills O2's spot in the box and O2 calls the name of another teammate. The offense must complete 10 passes without a turnover to win. On a turnover, defense switches to offense and offense switches to defense. Start at zero on each possession: must complete 10 consecutive passes.

Teaching Points	Be ready to make the pass when your teammate gets open; take away the defender's angle to the ball; use the stationary offensive players as screens; be physical; be strong with the ball.

Drill: The Gauntlet

Objective	To see the whole floor and create passing lanes to advance the ball down court.
Pre-Requisites	V-cut; L-cut; ball fake; pass fake; the Box; Diamond the Ball; and lay-ups.
Drill Execution	Divide the court into 4 zones – baseline to foul line extended; foul line to half court; half court to foul line; and foul line to baseline. Place two defenders in each zone; defenders cannot leave their zone. Two offensive players start on the baseline and attempt to get the ball to the other basket and score. On any defensive rebound, steal, turnover or out-of-bounds, the offense sprints to the beginning and tries again. If they score, the defense runs. Each pair goes for 2-5 minutes.
Teaching Points	Pass and cut – limit the dribbling; create manageable passing lanes; use pass fakes to move the defense and ball fakes to create a passing lane; and follow your shot.

To work specifically on V-cuts, passing and receiving, use the *2v0 Pressure Passing Drill* and build to the *2v2 Pressure Passing Drill* and then the other games.

Chapter 4: **Transition Basketball**

University of Tennessee Head Coach Pat Summit says "Basketball is a game of transition and you must practice transition basketball." Transition basketball dominates youth basketball games. This chapter covers offensive transition (fast break) and defensive transition (full court press). In youth games, many teams press, and presses lead to transition basketball: the offense breaks the press and creates a numbered advantage or the defense steals the ball and attacks with an advantage.

Full court, small-sided games give players more room to practice their skills and use the same skills required in 5v5 games and half court play. The advantage/disadvantage scenarios prepare players for these situations in upcoming games, and prepare players to make the right decisions in other "broken play" situations, like dribble penetration or rotations out of a double team.

Transition plays are the easiest way to build offensive confidence because of the open space and numbers advantage. The defense is disorganized, and the offense learns to attack the defense's weakest point. When the defense is set, the offense must choose the right tactics and strategy to disrupt or disorganize the defense to return to the "broken play" situation where the offense has the advantage (Villepreux).

To develop skills and build confidence, start with transition situations and build to half-court play. Transition basketball is unscripted. Well-coached teams play well in transition because it illustrates the coach's teaching during practice. Teams need principles to guide them in transition, but, ultimately, successful transition basketball relies on the offensive players reading the game, making the right decision and finishing the play with technical skill.

2v1 FAST BREAK

Golfers say that no two shots are exactly the same. In basketball, no two plays are exactly the same. Therefore, variable or random training best prepares players for game situations. Modified and small-sided games closely resemble the game environment and guarantee transition situations.

A 2v1 break develops through several scenarios:

1. Two offensive players attack together against one defensive player protecting the basket (i.e. pass over a trap to two offensive players at half court who attack the defense's safety).
2. An offensive player attacks a defensive player ahead of the pack and the second offensive player hustles to help his teammate (i.e. a steal occurs near half-court and the defense immediately picks up the offensive player and defends 1v1).
3. Two offensive players attack two unsettled defenders ahead of the pack (i.e. a quick outlet off a rebound catches the defense retreating too slowly).

Each of these scenarios creates a different attack. If one player is far ahead of the other, pass to the lead player for a 1v0 or 1v1 break and trail to the rim: always be the second man in case a teammate misses. To teach the 2v1 attack, however, use the following general guidelines:

- Run outside the lane-lines to spread the court, but not waste time;
- Dribble at the elbow with your inside hand to create an easier pass;
- Attack to score, not to pass;
- Make the defender commit. If the dribbler cannot read the front of the defender's jersey, finish;

- The other offensive player trails a step behind the ball handler outside the lane-line;
- If the defense commits to the ball and completely takes away the lane to the basket, make a bounce pass by the defender's feet against his momentum;
- After the pass, veer away to avoid a potential charge.

A 2v1 break is like a 1v0: finish with a lay-up every time. If the offense spreads the court and the ball handler attacks aggressively, a single defensive player should not stop two players. Mistakes occur when: (1) the ball handler attacks passively, and the defender takes away his passing lane, forcing him to shoot; or (2) the player without the ball runs too far ahead and becomes a stationary target, making it easier for the defender to stop the ball and recover. Otherwise, the offense should finish with a lay-up and have offensive rebounding position.

Games

I use three games to create 2v1 fast breaks: *1v2/2v1*, *Rabbit* and *2v2 Rugby*. *1v2/2v1* and *2v2 Rugby* also train handling the ball against a trap. For young players, *2v2 Rugby* is my favorite game because the players have plenty of space to practice their technical skills (ball handling, full speed lay-ups), while it creates realistic transition situations when the offense breaks the trap. Young players need more space to practice their developing technical skills, while advanced players need practice in tight spaces to develop better skills (Launder). These games introduce basic transition plays and provide a starting point to observe and assess players' technical and tactical execution.

Game: 1v2/2v1

Objective	To remain patient under pressure, protect the ball and make a move to advance the ball up court.
Pre-Requisites	V-cuts; L-cuts; speed dribble; protect dribble; space dribble; crossover move; pull-back crossover move; lay-up; power lay-up; and crossover lay-up.
Drill Execution	One player starts on offense, and two players start on defense. A coach or player inbounds the ball to the offensive player. The offensive player cuts to create a passing lane. Once he receives the pass, he attacks the defense. The defense denies the inbounds pass and tries to prevent the offensive player from getting the ball. If the offensive player gets the ball, the two defenders trap the ball and try to force a turnover or steal the ball. The offense tries to score at his offensive basket. On a change of possession (turnover, steal, made basket), the defense becomes the offense, attacking 2v1, and the offensive player defends. Play to two baskets; go to the end of the line; and switch the offensive player on the next turn.
Teaching Points	Start away from the ball and break to the ball – do not start on top of the baseline; feel the defense and protect the pass; stay to the middle third of the court – do not run to the corner; pick the weaker defender and attack his outside shoulder; do not turn your back on the defenders – no spin dribbles; use a space dribble to square up the defenders and attack again; cut off the defenders' angle of recovery.

Game: Rabbit	
Objective	To train open court ball handling and teach aggressive rebounding.
Pre-Requisites	Speed dribble; lay-up; power lay-up; chest pass; and bounce pass.
Drill Execution	Team A and Team B form lines on opposite sidelines at half court. A1 and A2 start at half court on offense while B1 starts on defense. After the ball crosses the half court line, B2 touches the center circle and sprints back on defense. Everything is live including a made basket: the defense must rebound or steal the ball to gain possession, and the offense can rebound a made basket and score again. Once Team A crosses half court, A3 retreats to the opposite end to become the first defender. After Team B gets the rebound or steal, A1 and A2 exit to the back of the line, and B1 and B2 attack the other basket 2v1. Once they cross half court, A4 sprints into the play as the trailing defender and B3 retreats to defense. Play to nine baskets.
Teaching Points	Spread the floor wider than the lane-lines; attack together with the non-ball handler trailing a step behind the ball handler; score quickly – zero or one pass; attack the glass for the rebound – make or miss.

Game: 2v2 Rugby	
Objective	To handle backcourt traps, create transition baskets and finish lay-ups under pressure.
Pre-Requisites	V-cuts; L-cuts; speed dribble; protect dribble; space dribble; crossover move; pull-back crossover move; lay-up; power lay-up; and crossover lay-up.
Drill Execution	Divide players into two-man teams; works best with eight players divided into four two-man teams. Game is 2v2. Stay on the court until someone scores against you. When the offense scores, they play defense against a new offensive team who inbounds the ball after the made basket. After the inbounds pass, the offense cannot pass the ball forward in the back court. An offensive player can dribble forward or pass backward. The defense pressures the ball handler and looks to trap along the sidelines. Once the ball passes half court, play with no restrictions. All out of bounds go to the defense. When the offense scores, the defensive pair moves to the end of their line. Play to five baskets.
Teaching Points	Defense: "trap the back pocket" – if the offense turns his back and dribbles laterally, the on-ball defender cuts off his lane and the off-ball defender traps from behind in his blind spot; see the floor – keep head and shoulders directed to the offensive basket; once a defender gets you moving toward the sideline, use a space dribble to separate and square to the basket; stay off the sideline; on a ball reversal, explode up court with a speed dribble; attack the basket; draw help and dish or finish 1v1.

Practice

When observing players during the small-sided games, decide on the cause of the errors:

- Were the players in the right position?
- Did the players make the correct decision?
- Did the players make technical mistakes (miss a lay-up, travel, etc.)?

The answers to these questions dictate the practice drills:

- Problems with proper positioning are tactical problems. The players likely need a short review on the proper spacing and more repetitions in the games or in a less complex drill. These are the first mistakes to address.
- Problems with decision-making are more complex. Use questions as a teaching tool to understand the players' mistakes. Young players may just need more experience in these situations to improve. Ask players what they saw or ask why they made the decision. The answers reveal the information needed to help the players improve. If the player never saw a trailing defender who stole the pass, the passer needs more court awareness; he might need more ball handling practice to develop more confidence with the ball so he sees the whole court rather than a narrow focus. If he saw the defender, he may need to improve his pass selection or practice passes with his weak hand off the dribble. Asking questions forces the player to think about his mistake and think about a better alternative rather than putting his head down and feeling bad about the turnover or forgetting it like nothing happened, and the coach gets more information to use in planning his practice blocks.
- Technical mistakes require more instruction and drills to learn the skill. Use a progression of drills to load the skill. Start with a drill which the players complete successfully and load the skill until the drills are game-like. For instance, if players missed too many lay-ups, choose the technique to address: the form of the lay-up, the coordination moving from the pass to the finish, balance on the shot, etc. Start with a simple drill and make it more and more complex before returning to the game form. A sample progression might be:
    1. Full Court Speed Lay-up
    2. Full Court Speed Lay-up with a defensive chaser
    3. Full Speed Lay-ups off the catch
    4. Full Speed Lay-ups off the catch with a help defender applying a little pressure/contact on the shot.
    5. Small-sided/Transition games

Some common problems or mistakes in 1v2, 2v1 and 2v2 situations are:

- Misreading the defender
- Attacking passively
- Taking a poor angle to the basket
- Missing the pass
- Missing the lay-up
- Not handling the back court trap
- Inability to beat a single defender with an open court move

Problem: Misreading the defender

Solution: More experience. Use the same games, or use drills like *2v2 Army Drill*, *2v2 Foster's Drill* and *2v1 Penetrate & Finish Drill* to get more repetitions in a short amount of time.

Drill: 2v1 Penetrate & Finish Drill

Objective	To read a help defender and make the correct decision (pass or finish); finishers work on a pivot and power lay-up to protect the ball.
Pre-requisites	Speed dribble; bounce pass; power lay-up; lay-up.
Drill Execution	One offensive player (O1) starts at the guard spot (lane-line extended beyond the three-point line) and the other (O2) starts on the opposite block. One defender (D1) starts in the key with one hand able to touch O2. O1 penetrates to the basket. D1 steps to help position – his objective is to stop the offense from scoring. O1 reads D1 and finishes with a lay-up or passes to O2. If he passes, O2 must finish. O1 becomes the next defense, D1 replaces O2 and O2 grabs the ball and returns to the end of the line.
Teaching Points	Read the defender's shoulders: if the defender does not commit all the way so the ball handler can read his jersey, the ball handler finishes; never jump to pass – make the pass early if the defense commits or finish; penetrate to score, not to pass – passing is the second option.

Drill: 2v2 Army Drill

Objective	To attack quickly and score before the second defender recovers; to finish lay-ups under pressure.
Pre-Requisites	Speed dribble; lay-up; power lay-up; chest pass; and bounce pass.
Drill Execution	Two offensive players start on the baseline and two defensive players start across from them along the free throw line extended. Throw the ball to one of the offensive players: the offense attacks 2v1. The corresponding defensive player (player across from player who received the ball) must touch the baseline and then get back on defense. The other defensive player slows the offense until his teammate recovers. Play until the offense scores or the defense gets a rebound or steal.
Teaching Points	Spread the floor wider than the lane-lines; attack together with the non-ball handler trailing a step behind the ball handler; score quickly – zero or one pass.

Drill: 2v2 Foster's Drill

Objective	To read a defender's positioning in the open court and make the appropriate tactical decision while attacking full speed.
Pre-requisites	Speed dribble with both hands; hesitation move; in-n-out move; crossover move; lay-up; power lay-up and crossover lay-up.
Drill Execution	Two offensive players start on the baseline and two defenders start at the free throw line with a ball. A defender passes to an offensive player, and the defenders sprint to half court, turn and play defense. The offensive player receives the pass, and they attack the opposite basket. The offense gets one shot only. Go to the end of the line and switch offense and defense on the next turn.
Teaching Points	Straight-line drive is better than a change of direction; attack the defender with speed and put him on his heels; stay off the sideline – allow space to go around a defender to the sideline side; attack at 80% speed so you can accelerate past a defender if necessary; once you beat the defender, cut off his angle of retreat; beat one defender and draw the second defender – if the help defender plays both offensive players, finish.

Problem: Made a bad pass.

Solution: Eliminate the defender and work on the timing between a passer and receiver on the run.

Drill: Celtic Fast Break Drill

Objective	To finish lay-ups directly from a pass at full speed and to time the pass to a teammate filling the lane.
Pre-requisites	Speed dribble; jump stop; push pass; stride stop; power lay-up; reverse lay-up.
Drill Execution	Form a line under each basket and an outlet line for each basket. Player 1 tosses the ball off the backboard (subsequent players rebound the previous shot) and throws the outlet pass. P1 fill the outside lane, running wide while P2 dribbles to the middle (This happens simultaneously at each end). P2 stops at the three-point line and passes to P1. P1 receives the pass, stops with a stride stop and finishes with a power lay-up. P2 slides toward the side of the pass.
Progression I	P2 stops at three-point line and passes to P1 at the three-point line. P1 catches and penetrates to the basket for a lay-up. P2 loops behind the drive.
Progression II	P2 stops at the three-point line and passes late to P1 filling the lane. P1 catches and shoots a reverse lay-up.
Teaching Points	Stop on-balance; pass with the outside hand; receive the outlet pass with butt to the sideline to see the whole floor; take your first dribble up the floor; go from the outlet to the top of the key in three dribbles.

Problem: Mishandled the pass.

Solution: Practice catching the pass using a stride stop and make different passes, including bad passes. Use the *1v0 Finishing Drill* with the coach passing and the *Celtic Fast Break Drill*.

- *Stride Stop*: A step-step stop where the first step becomes the pivot foot. Sit the hips back and down; flex the ankle, knee and hip to diffuse the force over a larger area and reduce the impact on any one joint. Stop with the lead leg knee over the foot. In this case, the stride stop is outside foot – inside foot. When running down the wing to the basket, the player opens his chest to the pass. As he catches, he steps down with his outside foot. On his next step, he turns his hips and shoulders to square to the backboard with feet pointing to the baseline. He jumps off two feet to finish a power lay-up.

Drill: 1v0 Finishing Drill

Objective	To gather and finish lay-ups in transition.
Pre-requisites	Stride stop; power lay-up.
Drill Execution	Coach stands at the free throw line and players start at half court. First player sprints toward the basket and the coach passes him the ball. The player catches the pass, stops with a stride stop and finishes a power lay-up. Work on different passes with different speeds and locations.
Teaching Points	Catch and gather; balance before jumping; square shoulders to the backboard; use the inside arm to protect the ball; catch the ball first – then concentrate on the shot.

Problem: Missed the lay-up.

Solution: Practice lay-ups at full speed and contested lay-ups in controlled drills. Load the skill from a breakaway lay-up to a game-situation lay-up. Use the progressions from the beginning of the chapter and drills like *1v0 Finishing Drill*, *Celtic Fast Break Drill* and *Open Court Lay-up Drill*.

Drill: Open Court Lay-ups

Objectives	To develop different change of direction moves and finishes at the basket.
Pre-requisites	Speed dribble; hesitation dribble; cross over progression; lay-ups.
Drill Execution	Start at half court and speed dribble toward the basket. At the three-point line, make a move. Attack the basket and finish. Mix up the moves (in-n-out, crossover, around-the-back, hesitation, double moves) and finishes (lay-up, power lay-up, crossover lay-up, reverse lay-up, inside hand lay-up).
Progression I	Have a defensive player at the basket for the offensive player to finish over.
Progression II	Use a pad or lightly slap the offensive player's arms as he finishes.
Progression III	Pair up with an offensive and defensive player. Defensive player starts on the baseline and offensive player starts at the free throw line-extended. Defensive player passes to the offensive player and chases the offensive player. The offensive player attacks the basket and finishes while preventing the defensive player from catching up and stealing the ball or blocking the shot.

Teaching Points	Change levels – get low as you explode past a defensive player; protect the basketball on the move – get the inside shoulder down; use speed to your advantage – a straight line drive is preferable to a change of direction, if possible; use your strength on the finish – if quickness is your advantage, jump off one foot; if strength or size is your advantage, jump off two feet.

Problem: Struggled with the backcourt trap.

Solution: Teach the pull-back crossover with the *Baseline Shuffle Progression* and use 1v1 and 1v2 drills to work on game ball handling against a pressure defender.

Drill: Baseline Shuffle Progression

Objective	To develop control with the ball while moving in different directions; introduce the *Space Dribble* and *Pull-back Crossover* used later.
Pre-requisites	Speed dribble; protect dribble; hockey stop; and crossover dribble.
Drill Execution	Start on the baseline with left foot forward and ball in the right hand by the right foot in a protect dribble stance (use the width of the body to protect the ball). Shuffle toward mid-court for three dribbles and then shuffle back to the baseline. Go for 30 seconds and then switch hands and practice with a left-hand dribble for 30 seconds.
Progression I	Sprint toward mid-court for three dribbles, stop with a hockey stop and shuffle toward the baseline in a protect dribble stance.
Progression II	Add the crossover dribble. Sprint toward mid-court for three dribbles, stop with a hockey stop and shuffle toward the baseline in a protect dribble stance. When the trail foot hits the baseline, drop the lead foot so your feet are parallel, cross over the ball and attack. With a right-hand dribble, drop your left foot when the right foot hits the baseline; cross over from your right to your left hand and step forward with the right foot as you sprint forward.
Teaching Points	Stay low; concentrate on quick changes of direction; push opposite the direction of intended movement; chin to your front shoulder – see the court.

Drill: Full Court 1v1

Objective	To develop confidence handling the ball under pressure.
Pre-requisites	Speed dribble; protect dribble; space dribble; crossover move; lay-up; power lay-up; and crossover lay-up.
Drill Execution	Offensive player starts on the baseline; defender checks the ball to the offensive player. The ball is live as soon as the offensive player picks up the ball. Offensive player attacks to the other basket; defender contains the dribble and attempts to force a turnover. Offense gets one shot to score. Pair goes to the end of the line and switches offense and defense on their next turn.
Progression I	Play to one basket. When the defensive player forces a turnover or gets a defensive rebound, he attacks the opposite basket. No out of bounds on loose

	balls. When finished, go to the end of the line and switch offense and defense.
Progression II	One player starts on each baseline. Coach tosses the ball. Whoever gets the loose ball plays offense and attacks the basket opposite his starting position, while the other player plays defense. Play to one basket. When the defensive player forces a turnover or gets a defensive rebound, he attacks his basket. No out of bounds on loose balls. When finished, go to the end of your line.
Teaching Points	Use a change of pace dribble to control the defender; minimize playing with the ball; keep shoulders squared to the basket – no side to side dribbles; attack the defender's lead shoulder if possible; cut off the defender's angle of retreat; and protect the ball on your finish – do not "rock the cradle."

Drill: 1v2

Objective	To remain patient under pressure, protect the ball and make a move to advance the ball up court.
Pre-Requisites	V-cuts; L-cuts; speed dribble; protect dribble; space dribble; crossover move; pull-back crossover move; lay-up; power lay-up; and crossover lay-up.
Drill Execution	One player starts on offense, and two players start on defense. A coach or player inbounds the ball to the offensive player. The offensive player cuts to create a passing lane. Once he receives the pass, he attacks the defense. The defense denies the inbounds pass and tries to prevent the offensive player from getting the ball. If the offensive player gets the ball, the two defenders trap and try to force a turnover or steal the ball. The offense tries to score at its offensive basket. Offense gets one shot. Return to the end of the line and switch offensive players on your next turn.
Teaching Points	Start away from the ball and break back to the ball – do not start on the baseline; feel the defense and protect the pass; stay to the middle third of the court – do not run to the corner; pick the weaker defender and attack his outside shoulder; do not turn your back on the defenders – no spin dribbles; use a space dribble to square up the defenders and attack again; cut off the defenders' angle of recovery.

Problem: Struggled to beat the defender 1v1 in the open court.

Solution: Simplify the drills to get more 1v1 repetitions. Use the *Foster's 1v1 Drill* and *Open Court Lay-up Drill* to practice different moves and finishes and the decision-making process against live defense.

Drill: **Foster's 1v1 Drill**

Objective	To read a defender's positioning in the open court and make the appropriate tactical decision while attacking full speed.
Pre-requisites	Speed dribble with both hands; hesitation move; in-n-out move; crossover move; lay-up; power lay-up and crossover lay-up.
Drill Execution	Offensive player starts on the baseline and the defender starts at the free throw line with a ball. Defender passes to the offensive player, sprints to half

	court, turns and plays defense. Offensive player receives the pass and attacks the opposite basket. Offense gets one shot only. Go to the end of the line and switch offense and defense on the next turn.
Progression I	Offensive player starts at half court and the defender starts at the top of the key. When the coach says, "Go!" the offensive player races to the opposite free throw line and the defender touches the baseline. The offensive player touches the opposite free throw line, turns and receives a pass from the coach. The defender touches the baseline and sprints forward. Offensive player attacks the basket; defender tries to prevent the offensive player from getting into the lane. Offense gets one shot.
Teaching Points	Straight-line drive is better than a change of direction; attack the defender with speed and put him on his heels; stay off the sideline – allow space to go around a defender to the sideline side; attack at 80% speed so you can accelerate past a defender if necessary; once you beat the defender, cut off his angle of retreat; and protect the ball on your shot – do not "rock the cradle."

3v1 FAST BREAK

A 3v1 Fast Break is similar to a 2v1 Fast Break, not a 3v2 Fast Break. Most often, players attack 3v1 with three players attacking simultaneously. The ball handler dribbles down the middle and a wing fills on either side. One of two things happens: (1) the ball handler dribbles into the middle because the defender never stops the ball; or (2) the ball handler stops at the free throw line and passes to one of the wings.

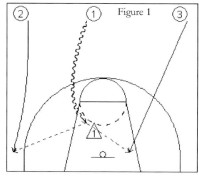

In a 3v1 Fast Break, the defender protects the basket. If the ball handler attacks the front of the rim because the defender never stops the ball, the court congests as the three offensive players converge. In the second option, the ball handler never draws the defender, so he waits for the pass and plays the receiver, contesting the shot and oftentimes forcing a second, late pass to the other wing.

Any time a 3v1 develops, turn it into a 2v1 with the third player flaring to the three-point line or trailing the play. If the ball handler picks a side and penetrates with the dribble, he should dribble to the side of the better shooter and away from the finisher (Figure 1). Worst case scenario, the shooter gets an open three-pointer. Best case scenario, the ball handler and the finisher attack 2v1 and get a lay-up.

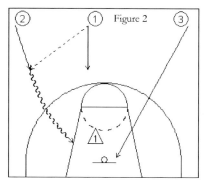

If the middle ball handler passes to one of the wings, the wings attack 2v1 (Figure 2). The middleman trails his teammates. If the wing passes too late to the other wing, the middleman can trail down the middle and receive a pass for a quick lay-up. Rather than attack 3v1, they create width and depth to attack the lone defender.

While counterintuitive, a 3v1 does not create an advantage over a 2v1 because a 2v1 should produce a lay-up every time. Oftentimes, the three-man break hurts spacing and makes it easier for the defender to do nothing and be reasonably effective. By spacing the floor with a 2v1 break plus a flaring shooter or a trailing middleman, the two players have an open teammate if a second defender retreats before the offense scores.

Questions to Resolve
1. Who is the better shooter and who is the finisher?
2. Should I pass ahead and trail or veer to one side and attack?
3. How can I make the defender commit to create a lay-up?
4. Where are the trailing defenders? Is it really a 3v1, or more of a 3v2?
5. What is the quickest way to get a great shot?
6. Are either of the wings playmakers, or should I keep the ball?

3v1 Fast Breaks occur in 3v2 games and drills, and the objective is to create a 2v1, so use the games and drills in the previous section. However, if you observe through the game play that you need to spend more time on the 3v1 break because players are not making the right decisions or not creating the proper spacing, use the *3v3 Army Drill* and use Progression I.

Drill: 3v3 Army Drill

Objective	To attack quickly before the third defender recovers; to finish lay-ups under pressure; and to make the right decision.
Pre-Requisites	Speed dribble; lay-up; power lay-up; chest pass; and bounce pass.
Drill Execution	Three offensive players start on the baseline and three defensive players start across from them along the free throw line extended. Throw the ball to one of the offensive players: offense attacks 3v2. The corresponding defensive player (player across from player who received the ball) must touch the baseline and then get back on defense. The other defensive players slow the offense until their teammate recovers. Play until the offense scores or the defense gets a rebound or steal.
Progression I	Start the same, with three offensive players and three defenders. If the ball goes to the middle person, drill remains the same. If the ball goes to one of the wings, both wings touch the baseline and retreat. The offense attacks 3v1.
Teaching Points	Spread the floor: wings along the sidelines; attack together; create a 2v1; score quickly – one or two passes maximum.

3v2 FAST BREAK

A 3v2 Fast Break develops through several scenarios, which create different alignments. Rarely do three players attack simultaneously against two defenders waiting in a tandem formation. Instead:

1. Three offensive players with the dribble in the middle of the court attack two defenders sprinting to the key to protect the basket in a tandem alignment.
2. Two offensive players attack two defenders scrambling to recover and protect the basket, while a third offensive player beats the other players down court to trail.
3. Two offensive players attack one defender and a second defender and third offensive player sprint into the play.

These are just three sample ideas. 3v2 Fast Breaks occur frequently, especially against pressing teams, but the alignment of the attack and the defenders is dynamic, not fixed, providing limitless options. The 3v2 Fast Break is also where a coach begins to outline his transition philosophy and build his secondary break. The ultimate decision is a middle break or a sideline break.

Teams that favor the middle break often outlet to the sideline, but the guard quickly dribbles to the middle. Middle break teams tend to favor one dominant point guard who serves as the primary playmaker. Teams that favor the sideline break use an outlet to the sideline and a second pass up the wing. They tend to relieve the pressure on a singular playmaker.

Many coaches favor the middle break because they limit the unknown: they trust their point guard – the designated playmaker – to handle the ball 90% of the time and serve as the primary decision-maker, while a sideline break gives each player equal opportunity. Since most coaches struggle to trust any player, trusting one designated point guard is easier than trusting the entire team to make the right decision. There are advantages and disadvantages to each:

Middle Break	
Advantages	**Disadvantages**
Uses the entire floor	Becomes 2v2 after first pass
Forces the defense to retreat to the middle	No defined cutter to the basket
Puts the ball in best decision-maker's hands	Indecision for wings – cut to the rim or flare
	Too much dribbling

Sideline Break	
Advantages	**Disadvantages**
Less traffic on the sideline	Narrows the court for the defense
Takes a defender away from the basket/middle	Dangerous to reverse ball through middle
Creates a 2v1 in the middle of the court	Slow developing: wait for a cut to the post
Post-oriented	Multiple decision-makers
Uses the pass more than the dribble	

As you choose your philosophy – middle or sideline, though every team uses both – there are several questions for a coach to consider:

1. Where do the wings go? Do they automatically cut to the basket or fade to the corner? Do they cut to the basket and continue to the other side of the court?
2. Who cuts to the rim? If the ball is on the wing, does the opposite wing cut through to the block? Does the outlet who passed to the wing cut to the basket? Is it always a post cutting to the rim?
3. Where does the post fill? Does he cut to the rim and then to the ball side to post?
4. Where does the trailer fill? Does he cut to the ball side? Does he cut to the weak side? Does he fill the opposite wing?
5. Where does the outlet/point guard go after passing to the wing?

> **Questions to Resolve (Ball Handler)**
>
> 1. Where is the opening?
> 2. What is the fastest and safest way to get the ball up court?
> 3. Who is with me? Can they handle the ball? Are they finishers?
> 4. In the scoring zone, do I pass early or hit the player right at the basket?
> 5. Can I beat the top defender and create a 2v1?
> 6. How can I get the bottom defender leaning in one direction to create an easy lay-up?
> 7. Are my teammates slashers or shooters? Will they cut to the rim or fade to the three-point line?

The answers help settle one's philosophy, though ultimately the game situation dictates the best play. If a coach teaches a middle break, but a wing is ahead of everyone with a 1v0 or 1v1 opportunity, the best play is to pass up the sideline to the wing, not dribble middle and jump stop at the free throw line.

These questions – and the coach's answers – form the transition principles for the team. Principles change as the situation dictates, but these give players a general template which enables them to expect certain actions or behaviors from their teammates. With the principles, players learn to play together, as the principles organize players around some basic concepts which enhance their performance.

> **Questions to Resolve (Non-Ball Handler)**
> 1. Do I cut to the rim or fade to the three-point line?
> 2. Do I catch and penetrate to the basket or wait for the cutter?
> 3. Do I cut and replace myself or cut through to the opposite side?
> 4. Do I cut to the ball side block or leave the area open for penetration?
> 5. From the weak side, should I cut to the basket or hold my position and space the floor on the weak side?

For instance, if the coach designs the break for the post to run to the rim and then post on the ball side, the point knows where to look for the post player and he knows to get the ball to one side of the court if they do not score with the first wave. He also knows that if he passes to the wing, the post fills the block rather than the point passing and cutting to the rim. He expects the post to fill that position. Without a set of principles, the point could pass and cut right into the post player cutting to the same spot. The principles serve as a guide, not an absolute.

Games

The games are similar to the 2v1 Games with an additional player. Once you have introduced all the different break scenarios, and want to use the games and drills to train the concepts, rather than introducing and teaching new skills, the drills and games provide an easy progression to move from 2v2 to 3v3 to 4v4 or 5v5 with the same basic rules. This adds efficiency to a practice setting as you review the rules one time for three or four drills, rather than teaching new rules every time you expand or change the drill.

Game: Rabbit

Objective	To handle the ball in the open court, rebound aggressively and make good decisions.
Pre-Requisites	Speed dribble; lay-up; power lay-up; chest pass; and bounce pass.
Drill Execution	Team A and Team B form lines on opposite sidelines at half court. A1, A2 and A3 start at half court on offense while B1 and B2 start on defense. After the ball crosses the half court line, B3 touches the center circle and sprints back on defense. Everything is live including a made basket: the defense must rebound or steal the ball to gain possession, and the offense can rebound a made basket and score again. Once Team A crosses half court, A4 and A5 retreat to the opposite end to become their first defenders. After Team B gets the rebound or steal, A1, A2 and A3 exit to the back of the line, and B1, B2 and B3 attack the other basket 3v2. Once they cross half court, A6 sprints into the play as the trailing defender and B4 and B5 retreat to defense. Play to nine baskets.
Teaching Points	Spread the floor wider than the lane-lines; attack together; score quickly; attack the glass; create a 2v1; attack the open space.

Drill: 3v2 Continuous Point

Objective	To practice the point guard's decision-making and the wings filling the lanes and finishing.
Pre-requisites	Speed dribble; lay-up; power lay-up; chest pass; and bounce pass.
Drill Execution	Divide players into pairs. Keep the point guards separate. Play a full court game, cut throat style: the winner of each possession stays on offense, the loser goes to the end of the line and the new team starts on defense. One point guard plays at a time and he remains on offense throughout the drill. Team A starts on offense and attacks Team B. If Team A scores, it grabs the ball, outlets to the point guard and attacks the other basket against Team C. If Team C gets a rebound or steal, Team C outlets to the point guard and attacks the other basket against Team D (or Team B if there are not enough players). Each individual team keeps track of its baskets. Play to five baskets and change the point guard.
Teaching Points	Make a play – do not just dribble to a spot; fill the lanes wide; attack the basket – do not settle; create 2v1 situations; attack the open space; force the defense to stop the ball.

Game: 3v3 Hockey

Objective	To handle backcourt pressure, create transition baskets and finish lay-ups under pressure.
Pre-Requisites	V-cuts; L-cuts; speed dribble; protect dribble; space dribble; crossover move; pull-back crossover move; lay-up; power lay-up; and crossover lay-up.
Drill Execution	Divide players into three-man teams; works best with 12 players divided into four three-man teams. Game is 3v3. Stay on the court until someone scores against you. When the offense scores, they play defense against a new offensive team who inbounds the ball after the made basket. The offensive team *must dribble the ball across half court* – no long passes. The defense pressures the ball handler and traps along the sideline. Once the ball passes half court, play with no restrictions. All out of bounds go to the defense. When the offense scores, the defensive pair moves to the end of their line. New team inbounds the ball and plays offense against the team that just scored. Play to five baskets.
Teaching Points	See the floor – keep head and shoulders directed to the offensive basket; once a defender gets you moving toward the sideline, use a space dribble to separate and square to the basket; stay off the sideline; on a ball reversal, explode up court with a speed dribble; attack the basket; draw help and dish or finish 1v1.

Game: 2v3/3v2

Objective	To remain patient under pressure, protect the ball and make a move to advance the ball up court.

Pre-Requisites	V-cuts; L-cuts; speed dribble; protect dribble; space dribble; crossover move; pull-back crossover move; lay-up; power lay-up; and crossover lay-up.
Drill Execution	Two players start on offense, and three players start on defense. A coach or player inbounds the ball to the offense. The offensive players cut to create passing lanes. Once an offensive player receives the pass, the offensive pair attacks the defense. The defense denies the inbounds pass and tries to prevent the offense from getting the ball. When the offense gets the ball, two defenders trap and try to force a turnover or steal the ball. The offense tries to score at its offensive basket. On a change of possession (turnover, steal, made basket), the defense becomes the offense, attacking 3v2, and the offensive players defend. Play to two baskets; go to the end of the line; switch offense and defense on the next turn.
Teaching Points	Start away from the ball and break back to the ball – do not start on the baseline; feel the defense and protect the pass; stay to the middle third of the court – do not run to the corner; pick the weaker defender and attack his outside shoulder; do not turn back on the defenders – no spin dribbles; use a space dribble to square up the defenders and attack again; cut off the defenders' angle of recovery; communicate and work together; space the floor; pass and cut aggressively; attack the basket.

Practice

When observing players play transition games, several mistakes occur frequently:

1. Too much dribbling
2. Pass too late – either the defense had recovered or the offensive player is flat-footed
3. Too congested – lack of spacing
4. Pass too early – (i.e. a post player not expecting the ball at the top of the key when he is sprinting to the rim)
5. Too slow developing
6. Pass to the wrong player – poor decision-making

Problem: Too much dribbling

Solution: Limit the number of dribbles. Use any of the games, but limit players to two or three dribbles each. Or, play any of the games, but use *3-2-1 Rules*: the first player has three dribbles to use; the second player has two dribbles; the third player has one dribble, and then the offense cannot dribble for the remainder of its possession. The objective is to get the ball moving.

Problem: Pass too late

Solution: Encourage the early pass. Players often play the drill, not the game. They learn to jump stop at the free throw line (three-point line), and they follow directions regardless of the situation. Rather than pass to the player cutting to the rim, they take one extra dribble to jump stop at the top of the key. Work on passing off the dribble and finding the open teammate as soon as he is open.

Problem: Too congested

Solution: If the key becomes too congested, the ball handler likely waited too long to pass or one of the wings did not read the ball handler's penetration and cut into his lane. Change the players' thinking from attacking 3v2 to creating a 2v1. If the two defenders sit back and protect the basket, find the shooter and make the open three-point shot.

Problem: Pass too early

Solution: Players must understand their teammates' strengths and weaknesses. Also, the ball handler must force the defense to play him before he passes. Just as there are occasions when a ball handler passes too late, sometimes players pass too early. They do not force the defense to stop the ball, which allows one defender to play two offensive players. Or, they pass to a player who is not ready to catch a pass and make a move. Teach players their teammates' strengths and weaknesses. The ball handler wants to put his teammates in a position to succeed, not to fail. Also, ball handlers need to be aggressive when the situation dictates. More experience coupled with feedback assists players in their development. Use questions to help players understand their mistake, rather than criticizing one player's skills to make a point to the passer ("Where is Jimmy most effective?" rather than "Jimmy cannot dribble, so why would you pass him the ball at the three-point line?").

Problem: Too slow developing

Solution: Use the shot clock. Give players a limited amount of time to shoot (7-10 seconds). The goal is to play fast, but also under control and to get good shots. However, to score in transition, players must make decisions at a faster pace.

Problem: Pass to the wrong player

Solution: Players need to know their teammates and read the defense. If players make the pass to the wrong player, they likely are not seeing the defender – they focus their attention on protecting the ball from their defender and making a move rather than seeing the whole court and finding the most open player. Develop players' confidence with the ball (Chapter 2) and use the games so players get more experience in transition situations.

4v3 FAST BREAK

When you reach the four-man break, concentrate on the width and depth of the players. In a two or three-man break, spread out the defense to create a lane to score. However, attacking with four people across congests the floor. Rather than attack with four players in one wave, create two waves. In a four-man break, the first wave is usually the three players and the second wave is the trailer. As the trailer enters the scoring zone, he reads the situation and cuts to open space.

> **Questions to Resolve**
> 1. What lanes should I/we fill?
> 2. Trailer: Where is the open spot?
> 3. Ball Handler: Where is our biggest advantage?
> 4. What is the defense's alignment? Where is the weak spot? Do they have one to stop the ball and the other two split the court? If we pull two to the strong side, can we create a 2v1 on the weak side?

Communication is underutilized offensively, especially in transition. As soon as a team outlets and sprints up court, one of the posts should yell that he is first post and he is filling the strong side block (or the designated lane). The second post reads his teammate and trails to the designated spot. If a player penetrates as the post gets to the scoring zone, the post reads the penetration and creates a passing lane. If he continues to fill the lane – if, for instance, the penetration is along the baseline – he can yell "Trailer!" to let the player know he has a new option available. Similarly, if the penetration occurs from the top, he can cut on the opposite side of the lane and yell "Trailer left!" or "Trailer right!" so the ball handler knows that he has another teammate available, which helps the ball handler "see" the whole court, including the players behind him.

Games

Game: 3v4/4v3	
Objective	To remain patient under pressure, protect the ball and make a move to advance the ball up court. To exploit transition situations and make the right decisions.
Pre-Requisites	V-cuts; L-cuts; speed dribble; protect dribble; space dribble; crossover move; pull-back crossover move; lay-up; power lay-up; and crossover lay-up.
Drill Execution	Three players start on offense, and four players start on defense. The offense inbounds the ball. The offensive players cut to create passing lanes. Once an offensive player receives the pass, the offense attacks the defense. The defense denies the inbounds pass and tries to prevent the offense from getting the ball. When the offense gets the ball, two defenders trap and try to force a turnover or steal the ball. The offense tries to score at its offensive basket. On a change of possession (turnover, steal, made basket), the defense becomes the offense, attacking 4v3, and the offensive players defend. Play to two baskets; go to the end of the line; switch the offensive players on the next turn.
Teaching Points	Start away from the ball and break back to the ball – do not start on the baseline; feel the defense and protect the pass; stay to the middle third of the court – do not run to the corner; pick the weaker defender and attack his outside shoulder; do not turn your back on the defenders – no spin dribbles; use a space dribble to square up the defenders and attack again; cut off the defenders' angle of recovery; communicate and work together; space the floor; pass and cut aggressively; attack with spacing and create a 2v1.

Game: 4v4 Transition	
Objective	To introduce the idea of width and depth in the team's spacing and to attack aggressively to create a 2v1.
Pre-requisites	V-cuts; L-cuts; speed dribble; protect dribble; space dribble; crossover move; pull-back crossover move; lay-up; power lay-up; and crossover lay-up.
Drill Execution	Play 4v4 full court with no restrictions. The offensive player who misses a shot or commits a turnover runs a lap around the entire court and then recovers into the play to create 4v3 fast breaks. Play to 5 baskets.
Teaching Points	Create width and depth; trailer cuts to an open spot; create a 2v1; use the whole court; find the open man early – no over-dribbling.

Practice

Many problems in a 4v3 or 5v4 break involve spacing, which is covered in more detail in the next chapter, or basic fundamental ideas and skills, which are covered in the 2v1 and 3v2 sections. The biggest difference is facing a diamond-type press with four defenders against three offensive players. Against back court pressure, players must be strong with the ball and exhibit patience. Pressure works when it forces the offense to make decisions and plays faster than the offense wants. By remaining patient, and relaxing under pressure, the offensive player can see the defense's vulnerabilities and attack accordingly.

If players struggle passing and receiving, review the games and drills in Chapter 3.

5v4 BREAK

In the five-man break, create width and depth: one wave should have three players and the other has two. The design of the break depends on the coach's transition philosophy. Most coaches run a numbered break: 1 is the outlet; 2 and 3 fill the wings; and 4 and 5 run the middle lanes. However, some coaches run more of a two-wave break: the first two players fill the wings and sprint to the rim; if they do not receive the ball, they run through and fill the opposite corner; the second wave runs the outside lanes, and fills to the basket. If neither wave creates a lay-up, the

---

Questions to Resolve

1. Is the defense forcing me into a trap?
2. Can I get the trapper to commit and pass to an open man before the defense's trap is set?
3. Can I attack the second defender before the trap is set?
4. Should I attack with a quick pass or the dribble?
5. Where is the defense's weakness?
6. Do I have space to split?
7. Is a teammate open?
8. Which teammate runs most aggressively to the ball?
9. Can I beat one of the defenders with the dribble?
10. Have I used my dribble?
11. Where are the help defenders lurking?

---

second wave can post or the point can set up the half court offense. It depends on the coach's philosophy, as many coaches run a structured secondary break based on their numbers. While their break is structured, players still need to understand the basics before adapting to the structured system.

In a 5v4 break, the offense has the defense disorganized and needs to find and attack the weak spot. Playing with a man advantage, whether 4v3 or 5v4, is like playing against a zone defense because the defense cannot match up man-to-man and cover all the offensive players. Therefore, the offense attacks by cutting to the open spaces, driving gaps and making the extra pass to the open player. If the offense has three players on the strong side, the defense has to decide how to defend: do they push three players to the strong side, match up man-to-man on the strong side and zone the two players with one defender on the weak side? Or, does the defense try to defend the three players with two and use two help defenders to defend he weak side and protect the basket? If the defense pushes three to the strong side, swing the ball to the weak side and attack with a 2v1 advantage; if the defense only pushes two to the ball side, find the open player for an open shot or drive a gap to draw two defenders and create a better shot.

On the other side, when the defense has the man advantage, the defense squeezes the space and makes it hard for the offense to find open players and passing lanes. At the youngest age groups, defenses shorten the court because the offensive players are not strong enough to throw hard, accurate passes the length of the court. For older players, practicing against a defensive advantage forces the offensive players to make sharper, more aggressive cuts and throw stronger, more accurate passes. When they face the same pressure 5v5, attacking the press is easier because they develop better habits against the additional pressure of a defensive man advantage.

The 4v5 pressure creates problems for an offensive team because the defense condenses the court and takes away angles which are available when the defense has two or three players. Teach the concept of *Diamond Spacing* as a principle for players to use when facing back court pressure.

Patience and spacing defeat pressure. When the defense traps, the ball handler needs patience, and his teammates need to create passing lanes. Most turnovers occur because the pressure causes the ball handler to make quicker decisions; his attention narrows and the area of his vision decreases, so he misses help defenders waiting to steal a lazy or ill-advised pass.

With the ball, the offensive player needs to relax and maintain his confidence and keep the ball active to protect it. Away from the ball, his teammates need to cut to *Diamond Spacing* to give him three passing outlets. Against a trapping defense, pass receivers must cut hard all the way to the ball. Once a player receives the pass out of the trap, he should look opposite for the next pass or attack with the dribble away from the trap.

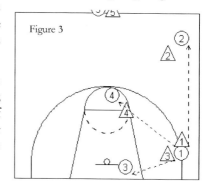

Figure 3

Diamond Spacing: When the defense traps a player, his teammates form a diamond: one teammate is ahead of the ball; one is behind the ball; and one is diagonal through the trap. If the defense traps and covers these three players, the fifth player runs to the front of the rim and is open for a lay-up. The basic principle organizes the attack and defeats pressure.

Games

Game: 4v5/5v4

Objective	To remain patient under pressure, protect the ball and advance the ball up court.
Pre-Requisites	V-cuts; L-cuts; speed dribble; protect dribble; space dribble; crossover move; pull-back crossover move; lay-up; power lay-up; and crossover lay-up.
Drill Execution	Four players start on offense, and five players start on defense. The offense inbounds the ball. The offensive players cut to create passing lanes. Once an offensive player receives the pass, the offense attacks. The defense denies the inbounds pass and tries to prevent the offense from getting the ball. When the offense gets the ball, two defenders trap and try to force a turnover or steal the ball. The offense tries to score at its offensive basket. On a change of possession (turnover, steal, made basket), the defense becomes the offense, attacking 5v4, and the offensive players defend. Play to three baskets and switch the advantage: four-man team adds a substitute, while the five-man team sits a player.
Teaching Points	Start away from the ball and break to the ball – do not start on the baseline; feel the defense and protect the pass; stay to the middle third of the court – do not run to the corner; do not turn your back on the defenders – no spin dribbles; use a space dribble to square up the defenders and attack again; cut off the defenders' angle of recovery; communicate and work together; space the floor; pass and cut aggressively; Diamond Spacing; look opposite the pressure; attack aggressively.

Game: 5v5 Transition

Objective	To introduce the team's secondary break philosophy.
Pre-requisites	V-cuts; L-cuts; speed dribble; protect dribble; space dribble; crossover move; pull-back crossover move; lay-up; power lay-up; and crossover lay-up.
Drill Execution	Play 5v5 full court with no restrictions. The offensive player who misses a shot or commits a turnover runs a lap around the entire court to create 5v4 fast breaks and then recovers into the play. Play to five baskets.
Teaching Points	Create width and depth; trailer cuts to an open spot; create a 2v1; use the whole court; find the open man – no over-dribbling; attack the defense's weak spot.

CONCLUSION

Some teams play transition basketball as an offensive system, while other teams are opportunists and run if they have an advantage, usually after a turnover. Regardless of the team's transition philosophy, some basic concepts remain constant:

1. Spread the floor and make the defense cover the whole court.
2. A 2v1 break is optimal.
3. Sprint the lanes.
4. Create horizontal (width) and vertical (depth) spacing. If initial thrust is thwarted, create space for the trailer.
5. Pass the ball ahead to an open player.
6. Do not pass the ball to a non-ball handler too early. Make the high percentage play. Do not ask players to make plays they are unaccustomed to making.

St. Louis University Head Coach Rick Majerus says, "Offense is spacing, and spacing is offense." When coaches preach teamwork, we picture passing and setting screens. However, good offensive spacing requires complete teamwork. To enhance the teamwork, teams rely on principles to guide players and improve their anticipation of their teammate's actions.

Teams initiate their offense from various alignments, but nearly every set maintains floor balance and 12- 15-feet of space between players. As the ball moves with the dribble or the pass, players adjust their position. As teammates move, players fill space and create open lanes.

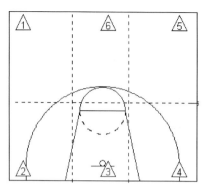

Mike MacKay, Basketball Canada's Director of Coach Education and Development, divides the court into six segments during his teaching sessions (right). No two players are allowed in the same segment. Will Robinson, a high school coach in Virginia, uses different perimeter spots; anytime the ball moves, players cut to a new spot and anytime a player runs past the post player, he screens for the post. These principles drive the coaches' motion offenses and the teaching behind their offensive systems.

CUT & REPLACE

A player without the ball reads the situation and makes the appropriate play to get himself open or to create a more dangerous opportunity for a teammate. Sometimes, a cutter does not intend to receive the pass, but instead cuts to move the defense and open a lane for a teammate or to create space for an offensive play. For instance, a post player on the block reads the direction of a teammate's drive and circles away from the area to give the ball handler a lane to the basket. At every moment, offensive players read their teammates and the defense to create more dangerous situations. On a middle pick-and-roll, the other post player vacates the low post, allowing the screener to roll to the basket, and fills to the high post; if he receives the pass, he has a high-low opportunity with the screener. The cut is not necessarily to get the ball or to create a shot for himself, but instead to give his teammates more space.

MacKay's six segments help to teach cutting and screening. However, an allowance must be made for a screener to enter into a segment with a player so the screen can be set. The other three players anticipate the screen and move to vacate the segments where the screener and the cutter are likely to cut. The ball handler and the off-the-ball players must resolve the following questions:

Ball Handler

- Do I have a driving lane?
- Can I use the dribble to create a shot for a teammate?
- Is a teammate open?
- Is a teammate in a more dangerous position (for instance, if I throw a skip pass to the opposite wing, will the low post have deep position in the paint)?
- Who has the best match-up? Who has the hot hand?

Off-the-Ball Players

- Am I in a dangerous position?

- Am I in a passing lane?
- Can I make a cut to clear the help defense and create a more dangerous position for a teammate?
- Can I cut to get open for a shot?
- Can I set a screen for a teammate?
- Can I clear the area for dribble penetration?
- Is the ball handler in trouble? Does he need someone to cut to relieve the ball pressure?

STRING SPACING

When a player dribbles in your direction, you have three primary options: (1) Flare; (2) Cut backdoor; or (3) Loop. Combining these three options with MacKay's six segments gives players a good idea of their teammates' motion and helps players to anticipate their teammates' cuts. The defense adds a variable, as everything ultimately depends on the defense, but spacing and location limit the defense's options.

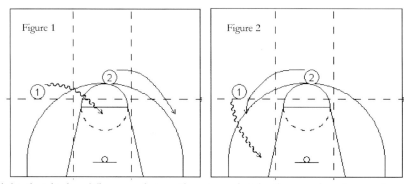

Imagine players are on a string: keep the string taut. If the player dribbles toward you, flare away from the dribbler to keep the string taut (Figure 1); if a player drives away from you, you loop behind to keep the string taut (Figure 2). This is an easy image for players to remember. They do not want the string to get too lax or so tight that it rips. They work together to maintain the spacing that makes an offense hard to defend.

The segments guide a player's cut. For instance, in the popular Dribble-Drive-Motion offense, does the man in the corner stay in the corner, loop behind the ball or cut backdoor? The answer depends on the defender, but also the level of the ball handler's drive.

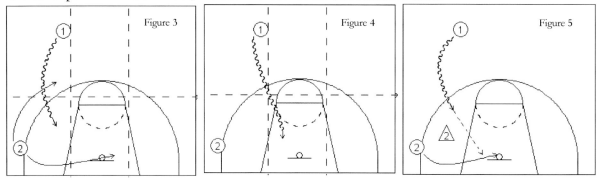

In Figure 3, P2 has two options: cut backdoor or loop behind the dribble. He has no more room to flare, and P1 is attacking into his segment. In Figure 4, P1 penetrates into the middle, so P2 can stay in the corner. The depth and location of the penetration forces a different response by the help defenders. In Figure 5, D2 helps "up" to stop P1's penetration, so P2 cuts backdoor. In Figure

6, D2 helps across to stop the penetration, so P2 loops behind the penetration. In Figure 7, the penetration draws D2 toward the middle of the court, and P2 is wide open. P2 reads the location of the drive to anticipate where to cut and then reads his defender to confirm the right cut. In Figure 6, for instance, if P2 cuts backdoor, he runs into his defender rather than separating from him, while in Figure 5, he cuts behind his defender to the basket. In a game, the player cannot read the dotted lines on the court; however, the segments help to teach players to read the situation and the level of the drive, so they make quicker and more accurate decisions in practice scrimmages and ultimately in the game. They learn to judge distances and timing.

As a perimeter player drives at a player on the low block, the post player must create an open lane. He has two choices: (1) if the drive is to the post player's bottom foot, he circles up the lane and to the middle (Figure 8); (2) if the drive is to his top foot, he circles away along the baseline (Figure 9). He keeps his shoulders square to the ball with his hands up to receive a pass.

As one player drives, his teammates relocate (Figures 10 & 11); if players stand and watch, the help defense's effectiveness increases. By moving, the offensive players force the help defenders to make choices. If the ball handler executes correctly and his teammates maintain their spacing, someone gets an open shot.

The player movement requires reading the drive's direction and the defender's reaction. However, good players anticipate and react immediately, while lesser performers take too long to make a decision. The players who anticipate and react have a "feel" for the game, while the lesser performers do not.

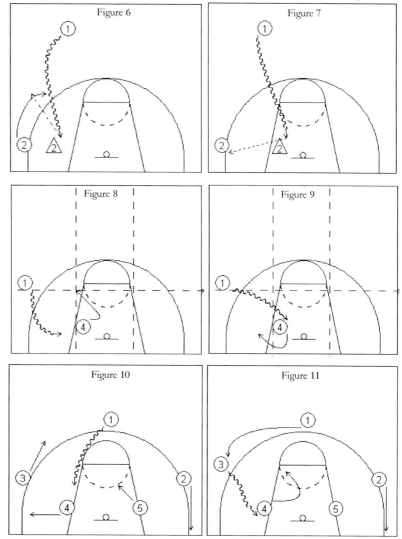

Figure 6

Figure 7

Figure 8

Figure 9

Figure 10

Figure 11

Questions for the Ball Handler to Resolve

1. What's my advantage vs. my defender?
2. Does the defense help all the way or bluff and recover?
3. Does a teammate have a hot hand or a big mismatch?
4. Where is the help coming from?
5. Did the defender "help up" or "help over?"
6. Is my teammate a shooter or a slasher?
7. Where is my outlet if I get stuck under the basket or in a trap?

To teach these concepts, use different small-sided games with modified rules to emphasize court spacing and dribble penetration. If players struggle with the movement, use the shooting drills to reinforce the proper decisions in drills and then return to the game action.

Game: 4v4 Cut Throat

Objective	To move after a pass and to square to the basket automatically.
Pre-Requisites	Hard2Guard position; pivot foot; cuts; lay-ups; bounce pass; chest pass; push pass.
Drill Execution	Divide the team into four-person teams. First team plays offense, second team plays defense and the other teams form a line on the baseline, ready to enter. The offense plays with two rules: 1. Square to the basket when you receive a pass 2. After passing, cut to the basket. Play until the offense scores or the defense forces a turnover, rebounds or the ball goes out of bounds. First team in line runs onto the court as the next defense and the winner plays offense: if the offense scores, they stay on offense; if the defense stops the offense, they move to offense. Loser goes to the end of the line.
Progression I	Play the same way, but limit the number of dribbles: each player gets two or three dribbles every time they catch.
Progression II	Play the same way, except only count assisted baskets. Use this if there is too much individual play and not enough teamwork.
Teaching Points	Cut hard; fill the open space; floor balance; attack the basket; use the whole floor; find the open man.

Game: 4v4 Canada Rules

Objective	To read the dribble penetration and make the appropriate decisions.
Pre-Requisites	*String Spacing*; speed dribble; push pass; hook pass; jump stop; catch-and-shoot shots; various finishes.
Drill Execution	Divide the floor into six sections: a horizontal line across the free throw line and two vertical lines which split the court into thirds. Play 4v4. Only one player is allowed in any section at one time. As a player penetrates from one section to another, the players move according to the *String Spacing* principles. If two players are in the same section, it is a turnover. Otherwise, play to score. If the offense scores, it stays on offense and new team enters on defense; defense must get a rebound or steal to move to offense.
Teaching Points	Go somewhere with the dribble; perimeter players move in circles; move to open passing lanes; rules prohibit screens; attack 1v1 to score – pass if you draw help; no standing still – every player adjusts to the ball as it moves.

Game: 4v4 Wildcat Rules

Objective	To penetrate and kick and finish around the basket.
Pre-Requisites	Speed dribble; push pass; hook pass; jump stop; catch-and-shoot shots; various finishes.
Drill Execution	Play 4v4. Players penetrate to the basket. If they cannot score, they pass to the open player. All passes must be received outside the three-point line. Catch and shoot or penetrate to the basket on the pass reception. If the offense scores, it stays on offense and new team enters on defense; defense must get a rebound or steal to move to offense.
Teaching Points	Penetrate to score; keep moving – keep your defender's attention to limit help defense; spread the court; be ready to shoot on the catch; catch squared to the basket; pass and space to the three-point line.

After watching the players play the modified games, determine the cause of the mistakes.

- Do players struggle to make the right decision with the ball?
- Do players move to the wrong areas?
- Do their technical skills break down?

Once you determine the cause of the breakdowns, use drills (the part) to teach and train these aspects of the skills and then return to the game action. *String Spacing Shooting Drill* and *I-Shooting Drill* train the basic motion in relation to dribble penetration and shooting off specific cuts. *2v2 Penetrate-and-Pitch Drill* isolates the decision making and gives the ball handler only one defender and one offensive player to read.

Drill: String Spacing Shooting

Objective	To review basic movement and spacing in relation to dribble penetration.
Pre-Requisites	Speed dribble; push pass; jump stop; catch-and-shoot shots.
Drill Execution	(1) *Flare*: Line 1 starts on the wing and Line 2 starts at the top of the key. L1 penetrates middle, and L2 flares away from the dribbler. L1 jump stops and passes to L2. L2 follows his shot and fills L1; L1 fills L2. (2) *Follow*: L1 attacks to the baseline side, and L2 loops behind. L1 jump stops and passes to L2. L2 receives the pass on the wing and shoots. L2 follows his shot, and L1 and L2 switch lines. (3) *Corner Outlet*: L1 starts on one wing and L2 starts on the other wing. L1 attacks to the baseline, and L2 drifts to the opposite corner. L1 passes to L2 who shoots. L2 follows his shot, and L1 and L2 switch lines.
Teaching Points	Penetrate to score, not to pass; catch with shoulders squared to the basket; move quickly, but do not rush; create open space for the drive and force the help defense to make a choice; do not allow one player to stop penetration and prevent the shot; show a target to the passer; hit the shooter in his hands; get feet set early for the shot.

Objective	To review the basic post player movement in relation to dribble penetration.
Pre-Requisites	Speed dribble; push pass; hook pass; jump stop; catch-and-shoot shots.
Drill Execution	One line (L1) starts on the wing and the second line (L2) starts under the basket. First player in L2 starts on the block. L1 attacks the paint from the baseline angle (L2's bottom foot); L2 floats up the free throw line. L1 throws a hook pass to L2. Next, L1 penetrates to the middle (L2's top foot) and L2 opens to the ball and drifts to the short corner. L1 passes to L2 and L2 shoots. L2 follows his shot and moves to L1, while L1 moves to L2.
Teaching Points	Keep shoulders squared to the passer; use a hook pass over the defense or a quick push bounce pass; catch ready to shoot or finish – anticipate the pass.

Game: 2v2 Penetrate and Pitch

Objective	To create a great shot through dribble penetration with a kick out to a shooter or a shot at the rim.
Pre-Requisites	Speed dribble; change of direction moves; *String Spacing*; catch-and-shoot shots; push pass.
Drill Execution	Divide the court in half and start with an offensive and defensive player at half court and an offensive and defensive player in the corner. O1 drives to the basket trying to score; if he draws the help, O2 makes the appropriate cut and O1 makes the pass. If he does not draw help, he should be able to create his own shot 1v1. Play until the offense scores or the defense gets a rebound or steal. Winner goes to offense, new team enters on defense and loser goes to the end of the line.
Progression I	Limit the offense to one pass. O1 has to create a shot for himself or a teammate.
Teaching Points	Attack North-South; make the easy play; force the help defense to commit.

POST SPACING

String Spacing involves movement away from the ball in relation to dribble penetration, while *Cut & Replace* organizes player movement in relation to basket cuts. The other general spacing concept to teach is movement away from the ball when the ball enters the low post. Many offenses stop when the post receives the pass on the block: the offense is designed to pass the ball there, and the assumption is that the player will score, so nobody concentrates on the other four players once the post receives the ball. This facilitates traps and double-teams in the post as offensive players stand and watch rather than cutting and making themselves hard to guard away from the ball. Offensive players need to treat a post entry pass as any other pass and move accordingly.

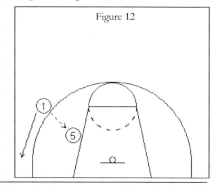

Figure 12

On the post entry pass, the passer has three general options: (1) relocate; (2) give-and-go; and (3) screen away. These concepts are covered in more detail in the following chapters, but they relate to general spacing concepts. To relocate, the player passes into the post and moves out of his defender's vision. For instance, if he passes from the wing, and his defender helps on the post with his back to the baseline, the passer drifts to the corner to relocate (Figure 12). When the passer relocates, the other players generally stand around or spot up on the weak side. To create more movement and make double teams more difficult, use one of the other two options.

On the give-and-go, the passer reads the spacing. If the post is above the first hash mark, the passer cuts to the baseline side; if he is below the first hash mark, he cuts above the post player (Figure 13). As he cuts, he needs to leave some space, rather than running directly past the post player. He is not looking for a hand-off; instead, if his man decides to stop and double, he is open for a quick pass. However, his main purpose is to vacate the space and take his defender to the weak side. When he cuts, the other players rotate and fill his space, just like with the *Cut & Replace*.

To set a screen, the passer cuts toward the elbow and screens for the next player (Figure 14). If his defender hedges or switches on the screen or decides to double the post, he cuts from the elbow to the front of the rim. After setting the screen, he can dive to the basket or flare to the three-point line.

If there are three players on the strong side when the ball enters the low post, both players cut. The players can cross (Figure 16), stagger their cuts (Figure 17 & 18) or cut straight ahead with the baseline player cutting along the baseline and the wing cutting to the elbow (Figure 15). Just as before, their teammates fill the vacated area on the ball side wing.

If the defense double teams the ball, the player whose man doubles must communicate and cut to an open space, preferably to the front of the rim. The other players create *Diamond Spacing*, so the offense can punish the double team with a lay-up or a wide open three-pointer.

In Figure 19, P1 passes to P5 and starts his cut to the basket. D1 stops and doubles P5. P4 replaces P1, just like with the basic *Cut & Replace* and P3 and P2 cut to *Diamond Spacing*. P3 and P2 can cut toward the ball to make shorter, safer passes or spread to the three-point line to spread the defense and create a wide

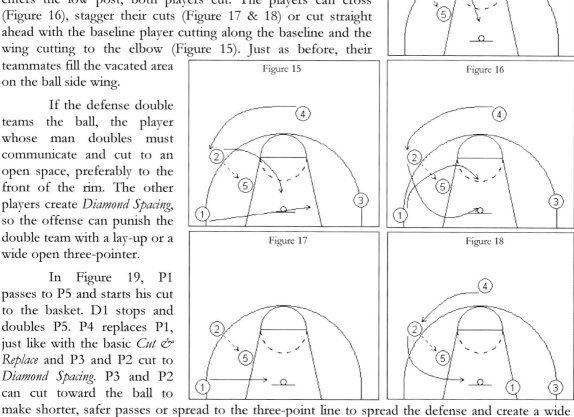

Figure 13

Figure 14

Figure 15

Figure 16

Figure 17

Figure 18

open three-pointer on a pass out of the trap.

The passes and the ball rotation depend on the defense's movement, but the offense spaces the floor to give P5 four options (Figure 20). With two players on the ball, someone has to be open. In a normal rotation, D2 or D4 switches to cover P1 since P1 is the biggest threat at the front of the rim. If D4 drops to take P1, there is nobody to pick up P4. If D2 rotates to P1, P2 is wide open in the corner or if he chooses to cut like in the diagram, P5 has a baseline side bounce pass to P2 for a lay-up. If D2 takes P1, D3 zones the weak side and is responsible for P2 and P3. Therefore a skip pass from P5 leads to an open shot for one of the players, typically P2 in the corner.

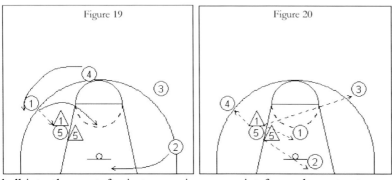

Figure 19   Figure 20

Games

Use *4v4 Cut Throat* or *4v5 Games* to practice ball and player movement when the defense traps on the low block. In *Cut Throat*, rather than play with a four-out alignment, use a three-out, one-in alignment; and reward the offense for getting the ball into the post; for instance, give one point for each post entry pass into the low block in addition to counting baskets or count any basket as two points if the offense scores off a cut related to low post play.

To play against a trap, force the defense to double team anytime the defense receives the ball on the low block. In 4v5, use the extra defender to trap on the low block. Also, to practice the full rotations, play 5v6 with the 6th man only there to trap on the low block.

Practice

After watching the players play, decide the cause of the mistakes:

1. Do the players forget where to cut?

2. Do they cut too close to the post player?

3. Is the post player in a hurry to make a move?

4. Does the post player struggle to make the pass out of the double team? Is the pass deflected by the trappers or does a help defender steal the pass?

If the problem is the general movement, use the basic spacing concepts to create shooting drills. If the problem is the passing under pressure, use the Chapter 3 drills to practice passing and receiving skills.

Conclusion

Understanding these basic spacing principles helps all teams, even those that run a lot of set plays or continuity offense. Within a set play, players will make individuals moves, whether passing into the post, breaking off a cut or penetrating with the dribble. If teams rely solely on set plays and have no other basic understanding, the individual plays are all or nothing: the player creates his own shot or his decision leads to a turnover or a bad shot. If players understand these basic principles of *Cut & Replace*, *String Spacing* and *Post Spacing*, they react to the individual play, maintain spacing and make it more difficult for the defense to prevent a good shot. Understanding these underlying principles make the following tactical skills more effective in games where the unpredictable happens.

While basketball is a 5v5 game, many sequences are simple two-man plays. The following three tactical skills utilize two players and good court spacing.

PASS & CUT/GIVE & GO

The give-and-go is the most basic fundamental tactical skill. One player passes to a teammate; he cuts and receives a return pass. The cut takes advantage of the defender's natural instinct, which is to relax. The offensive player cuts across the defender's face creating an easy return pass (Figure 1). If the defender reacts to the pass and jumps to the ball, the offensive player back cuts; the offensive player cuts opposite the defender's movement (Figure 2). If the defender sticks to the passer, the offensive player makes a V-cut to set up his cut (Figure 3).

Figure 1

Figure 2

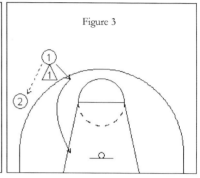

Figure 3

The give-and-go relies on four things:

1. Court spacing;
2. Reading the defense;
3. Squaring quickly;
4. Passing to the correct side of the cutter.

Court Spacing: The cutter needs space for the give-and-go. In the half court, most give-and-go cuts are basket cuts, meaning the rest of the team must leave a lane to the basket open.

Cutter Reads the Defense: The cutter has three options: (a) cut ball side; (b) cut backdoor; or (c) use a V-cut to set up a basket cut. If the defender stands flat-footed, cut across his face to the ball side and look for the return pass. If the defender jumps to the ball, cut behind the

> **Questions for the Cutter to Resolve**
> 1. How did my defender react to the pass?
> 2. Which cut is open?
> 3. Is the space open for a cut?
> 4. Is the passer ready?

defender. Finally, if the defender prevents an easy cut, use a v-cut. The V-cut can start in either direction and end with a back cut or a cut across the defender's face.

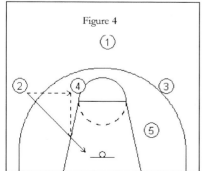

Figure 4

The V-cut is effective on a wing-to-high post pass. If the cutter steps toward the high post, the defender has to honor the cut and prevent the hand-off to the middle, leaving the backdoor cut open (Figure 4). Or, the cutter can cut low to fake the basket cut and cut over the top for the hand-off.

Square Quickly: Once the pass receiver catches, he squares to the basket. However, sometimes an automatic square is not quick enough. A late pass is the defender's only chance. Catch and square to the basket as quickly as possible; however, sometimes the best pass is the one not thrown.

Read the Cut: The passer must read the type of cut; did the cutter cut across the defender's face or cut backdoor? A backdoor cut requires a bounce pass leading to the basket because the defender is on the high side. On a cut across the defender's face, use an air pass because the defender is behind the cutter.

> **Questions for the Passer to Resolve**
> 1. Was the cut in front or behind the defender?
> 2. Do I have a passing angle?
> 3. Does a teammate have a better angle (i.e. ball reversal for a high-low)?
> 4. What is the cutter's strength? Should I wait for him to establish post position or pass early for a shot on the move?

If the passer cannot deliver a pass on time, hold the ball. Rather than make a late pass, allow the cutter to stop and establish post position. On a backdoor cut, the defender is on the ball side, top side, so a wrap-around pass into the low block leads the cutter to the basket for a power lay-up. On a cut over the top, the defensive player is caught behind, giving an easy angle for a post entry pass and a quick post move.

Games

Use *4v4 Cut Throat* to practice cutting to the basket after passing and squaring to the basket after receiving the pass. The game moves quickly and gives players numerous repetitions.

Game: 4v4 Cut Throat

Objective	To practice give-and-go cuts and squaring to the basket.
Pre-Requisite	Pivot foot; chest pass; bounce pass; V-cut; lay-ups.
Drill Execution	Cut Throat games involve multiple teams, at least three per basket. If offense scores, they stay on offense. New team sprints on the court as the defense. Old defense leaves the court and goes to the end of the line. If defense gets a rebound or a steal, they move to offense, and the offense goes to the end of the line. All out of bounds are rewarded to the defensive team. On any change of possession, the new offensive team must pass to the coach to check the ball. When the coach passes the ball to an offensive player, the ball is live.
Progression I	On any reception, player must pivot and square to the basket; otherwise, it is an automatic turnover. On any pass, the passer must cut to the basket; otherwise, it is an automatic turnover.
Progression II	Limit the number of dribbles on each pass reception to two or three dribbles.
Progression III	Count only assisted baskets.
Progression IV	No dribbling.
Teaching Points	Square quickly to the basket; cut hard; cut and replace; read the defense.

Practice

Use Cut Throat to teach the idea of cutting after a pass and pivoting to the basket. If players struggle, determine the cause of the mistakes:

- Does the cutter read his defender properly?

- Is the passer ready to make the pass?
- Does the passer make the wrong pass?
- Does the passer's defender deflect the pass?
- Is the spacing poor?
- Do the players miss lay-ups or open shots?

Use the *UCLA Cut Lay-up Drill* to train the cut, pass, reception and lay-ups. If players struggle to read the defense correctly, or if the passer's defender deflects too many passes, use the *3v3 Half Court No Dribble Game* to emphasize strong cuts and strong passing.

Game: 3v3 Half Court No Dribble

Objective	To make hard, aggressive cuts and pass under pressure.
Pre-Requisites	Pivot foot; V-cuts; bounce pass; chest pass; wrap-around pass; lay-ups.
Drill Execution	Divide the team into three-person teams. Play half-court with no dribbling allowed. If offense scores, they stay on offense. New team sprints on the court as the defense. Old defense leaves the court and goes to the end of the line. If defense gets a rebound or a steal, they move to offense, and the offense goes to the end of the line. All out of bounds are rewarded to the defensive team. On any change of possession, the new offensive team must pass to the coach to check the ball. When the coach passes the ball to an offensive player, the ball is live.
Teaching Points	Set up the cut; cut and replace; keep moving; be strong with the ball; be ready to make the pass; read your teammate's cut and anticipate the correct pass.

Drill: UCLA Cut Lay-ups

Objective	To finish lay-ups off the give-and-go cut; to develop the habit of cutting immediately after a pass and squaring immediately to the basket.
Pre-Requisites	L-cut; V-cut; power lay-up; lay-up; reverse lay-up; and bounce pass.
Drill Execution	One line (L1) starts at the block and the second line (L2) beyond the three-point line at the guard spot. First player in L1 makes an L-cut and receives the pass on the wing beyond the three-point line. First person in L2 passes to the wing and makes a basket cut. He receives the pass, finishes the lay-up and goes to the back of L1. The passer follows his pass, rebounds and goes to the end of L2.
Progression I	Add a help defender to apply light pressure to L2 as he catches and finishes.
Progression II	Add a form defender to L1; O1 cuts to the wing to receive the pass; D1 applies pressure, but does not steal either pass.
Progression III	Add a defender to L2: O2 passes and reads D2. Once O2 makes his cut, D2 trails and applies light pressure on the shot.
Progression IV	Add defense; Start with pass to the wing. Offensive players have one dribble. If players do not square to the basket or if passers do not cut immediately, it is a turnover. Play until the offense scores or the defense secures the ball. The winning team plays offense and new team plays defense; losers go to the end of the line.

Teaching Points	Lead the cutter with the pass – throw to the baseline side of the defender; time the cut – give the receiver a chance to pivot to the basket; be quick, but don't rush; catch with a stride stop or jump stop to finish; use ball fakes to create a passing lane.

DRIBBLE-AT

The dribble-at creates two options: (1) backdoor cut or (2) dribble hand-off. The ball handler initiates the play to keep off-ball offensive players from flocking to the ball. To execute a dribble-at:

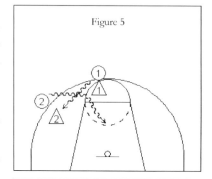

Figure 5

- Dribble at your teammate's defender;
- If the defender drops under the level of the ball, hand-off;
- If the defender plays between you and your teammate, your teammate cuts backdoor;
- To hand off, jump stop just short of his defender; hand the ball to your teammate at waist level, like a quarterback handing to a running back, and set a screen (Figure 5);
- On the backdoor cut, make a bounce pass directly from your dribble and lead your teammate toward the basket (Figure 6)

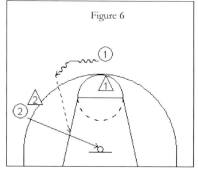

Figure 6

The dribble hand-off is a guard to guard or a post to guard exchange. On a guard to guard exchange, the original dribbler flares for a jump shot; on a post to guard exchange, the post rolls to the basket to take advantage of a switch or hedge by the defense.

Questions to Resolve

1. How is my defender defending me? Can I penetrate to draw help (or score) or am I penetrating at my teammate's defender for the hand-off?
2. How is my teammate's defender playing him?
3. Which way is the defender leaning?
4. Where is his weight?
5. Where are his eyes?
6. Is the post open for a backdoor cut?

Games

Use different 3v3 and 4v4 games like *4v4 Princeton Rules* and *3v3 Weave* to develop the dribble-at skill.

Game: 4v4 Princeton Rules

Objective	To emphasize the dribble-at and open backdoor cut lay-ups.
Pre-Requisites	Passing off the dribble; jump stops; lay-ups.
Drill Execution	Offensive players must stay above the free throw line extended excepts cut to the rim; if the player does not receive the pass, he fills the opposite wing. All baskets count, but count baskets on a backdoor cut as two points. Play until the offense scores or the defense secures the ball. Winner plays offense, loser goes out and

	new team enters on defense. When the coach passes to the offense, the ball is live.
Teaching Points	Make the bounce pass off the dribble; jump stop on the hand-off; set up a cut; *String Spacing* – follow the drive.

Game: 3v3 Weave

Objective	To emphasize the dribble-at and open backdoor cut lay-ups.
Pre-Requisites	Give-and-go; passing off the dribble; jump stops; lay-ups.
Drill Execution	Play 3v3 half court. All offensive plays must initiate with a dribble-at. If a player cuts backdoor and the pass is not made to the cutter, the only other option available is a give-and-go cut. Play until the offense scores or the defense gets a rebound or steal. Winner goes to offense, loser goes out and new team enters on defense. When the coach passes the ball to an offensive player, the ball is live.
Teaching Points	Make the bounce pass off the dribble; jump stop on the hand-off; set up a cut; string spacing – follow the drive away from you.

Practice

If players struggle to read their defender, the game bogs down, as one player dribbles side to side. The ball should move crisply, either with the hand-off or the backdoor pass. If a player dribbles from the middle to the wing and the wing cuts backdoor but is not open, another player should fill behind the dribbler adhering to the *String Spacing* principles. Also, after the backdoor cut, the cutter can reverse pivot and seal on the block. On a pass to the block, the offense reverts to its *Post Spacing* concepts.

If the ball handler reverses, use a give-and-go cut. If the cut is not open, reverse the ball all the way with the dribble so the ball is not stuck on one side of the court. Even though the rules restrict the offensive players, they need to be creative in order to create shots. If players struggle to make the right reads, they may need more experience; use a quick explanation and keep playing, or use the *Dribble-at 1v1 Drill* to practice reading the defender. If the mistakes are technical – poorly paced or located passes, missed lay-ups – use the *Dribble-at Lay-up Series* to practice the technical aspects of the hand-off and backdoor pass. The one-hand off-the-dribble pass requires attention because there is a small window to fit the pass. In the *Dribble-at Lay-up Series Drill*, use cones to give players a target for the pass; if they cannot fit the pass through the window, they should continue to the wing and look for the reverse pivot and seal, rather than forcing a bad pass.

Drill: Dribble-at Lay-up Series

Objective	To develop the backdoor bounce pass, the hand-off and finishing at the basket.
Pre-Requisites	Power lay-up; lay-up; reverse lay-up; crossover lay-up; floater; spin lay-up; up-and-under; bounce pass; V-cut.
Drill Execution	First line (L1) starts above the top of the key and second line (L2) starts on the wing. L1 dribbles at L2; L2 cuts backdoor and L1 makes a one-hand bounce pass off the dribble. L2 finishes: (1) power lay-up; (2) lay-up; (3) reverse lay-up. Next, L1 dribbles at L2, jump stops and hands the ball to L2. L2 attacks the rim: (1) crossover lay-up; (2) floater; (3) spin lay-up; (4) up-and-under.

Progression I	L1 starts above the top of the key, L2 starts on the wing and L3 starts above the guard spot with a ball. L1 dribbles at L2, jump stops and hands the ball to L2. L2 attacks the rim: (1) crossover lay-up; (2) floater; (3) spin lay-up; (4) up-and-under. L1 rolls to the basket/pops to the corner and receives the pass from L3: (1) power lay-up; (2) lay-up; (3) jump shot; (4) one-dribble jump shot.
Teaching Points	Bounce the ball at the defender's feet on the backdoor pass; quick push pass – no wind-up or extra motion; attack under control; jump stop on the hand-off.

Drill: Dribble-at 1v1

Objective	To read the defender's positioning and make the right cut.
Pre-Requisites	Protect dribble; hesitation dribble; lay-ups; shot off the dribble.
Drill Execution	Form a line at the top of the key with an offensive player and a defender on the wing. The two players play 1v1; to get the ball, the first person in line dribbles at the offensive player. The offensive player reads his defender and cuts behind for the hand-off or backdoor for the bounce pass. The offense gets three dribbles and one shot to score. The passer goes to defense and the winner plays offense – if the defense stops the offense, he plays offense; if the offense scores, he stays on offense.
Teaching Points	Set up the defender with a hesitation and read the defender's reaction; if the defender goes under the hand-off, be prepared to stay behind the screener and shoot; attack aggressively; get body low on the hand-off and turn the corner.

PICK & ROLL

Some coaches do not like to teach an on-ball screen to young players because young players naturally flock to the ball. However, the on-ball screen is the easiest screen to set, and the most likely screen for the screener to receive a pass.

On a screen away from the ball, the screener must find the right man to screen. For experienced players, this is a non-issue, but an inexperienced player must remember when to set a screen, where to set the screen, how to set a screen, and who to screen, as the defender is in help position. This combination leads to mistakes. The on-ball screen eliminates some ambiguity because the man to screen is guarding the ball.

Questions for the Screener to Resolve
1. How is my defender defending me? Is he cheating and giving me the slip to the basket?
2. Should I pop or roll?
3. Where should I cut if the defense traps?
4. Where is the open space on the roll to the basket?
5. Will my defender recover to me or do they rotate another defender to me?

The best way to entice players to set screens is to reward the screener with the ball. If a player sets a good screen, he gets himself open. However, young players focus on one player; they do not see the cutter and the screener. Due to inexperience, their attention narrows, especially if the defense applies pressure. They focus on the cutter because he is *supposed* to receive the pass. If the screener never receives a pass, he gets no credit for his effort. In an on-ball screen, the screener gets the ball more often because the ball handler focuses on the roller as he is *supposed* to get the ball.

Set an on-ball screen within the ball handler's shooting range so the defense cannot go under the screen. Spacing is critical: If the ball handler turns the corner, but another player is there, the offense loses its advantage; if the ball handler draws two defenders, the screener needs an open area to roll to the basket. Use the court segment concepts to keep the floor spread.

When using the screen, the ball handler should get low to protect the dribble and go shoulder to hip with the screener. The screener sets a strong, wide screen. The ball handler must run his defender into the screen. The first option is the ball handler turning the corner and getting into the lane for a shot or pass. The ball handler must attack with this mindset and not decide to pass before the play develops. Most importantly, the screen must disrupt or disorganize the defense by opening a lane for penetration or forcing a switch and a mismatch or the screen is ineffective.

Questions for the Ball Handler to Resolve
1. How is my defender playing me?
2. How is the screener's man defending him?
3. Does the screener pick and pop or roll to the basket?
4. Where are my teammates? How is the floor spaced?
5. From what direction did the help come?
6. How does the defense rotate?

The two most popular on-ball screens are (1) the high on-ball screen set in the middle of the court above the top of the key (Figure 7) and (2) the side on-ball screen (Figure 8). On-ball screens in the back court congest the space and increase a defense's ability to trap and pressure the ball, so I discourage their use.

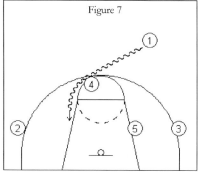

Figure 7

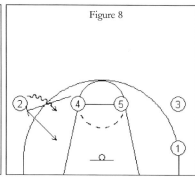

Figure 8

(1) High On-ball Screen

- Set screen near the top of the key;
- Screener squares his chest toward the ball handler;
- Screener's back faces where you hope to get the player open.

A flat screen makes it difficult for the screener's defender to hedge or help (Figure 9). In the flat screen, the ball handler attacks down the middle and the screener faces half court. The Miami Heat, with Dwyane Wade, is the best example of the flat screen. This is a more advanced high on-ball screen.

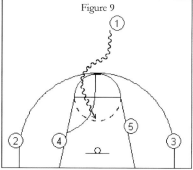

Figure 9

When using a more traditional high on-ball screen and attacking from an angle:

- Attack hard with the defender on your hip and run him into the screen (Figure 10);
- Dribble with the inside hand in a protect dribble stance, walk the ball below the level of the screen and attack horizontally (Figure 11); or
- Attack away from the screen, change directions and attack the screen (Figure 12).

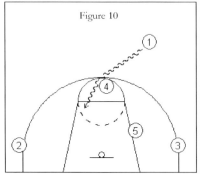

Figure 10

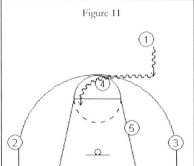

Figure 11

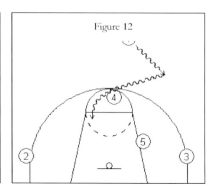

Figure 12

(2)The Side Pick-and-Roll: Take the defender below the level of the screen, so the screener gets the right angle (Figure 13). If the defense hedges hard or traps, pass to the middle and then the screener. Attack aggressively, but show patience against a switch (Figure 14).

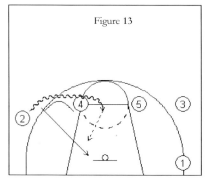

Figure 13

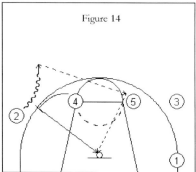

Figure 14

Using an On-Ball Screen

Attack the on-ball screen to turn the corner and get to the basket. However, the defense dictates the right play. If the ball handler's defender gets caught on the screen or goes over top, turn the corner and force the screener's defender to stop you. If you cannot beat the hedging defender immediately, use a fan dribble to create space. A fan dribble is a lateral shuffle dribble with shoulders squared to the basket. If the screener's defender offers no resistance, attack the rim.

Defense Goes Under – No Hedge

If the ball handler's defender goes under the screen, and the screener's defender does not hedge, square your shoulders and attack down hill. Do not let the defense off the hook; attack your defender and make him stop the ball.

Defense Hedges

If the screener's defender hedges use at least two dribbles to extend the hedge (Figure 15). The cardinal sin of pick-and-roll basketball is to pick up the dribble. If the hedge is flat (defender keeps his back to the baseline) or soft (steps out

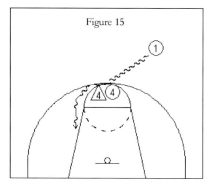

Figure 15

with a hand and a foot, not his whole body), stay low and attack the hedge, using the two dribbles to turn the corner. Best case, you beat the hedge and turn the corner; worst case, the hedger prevents you from turning the corner, but you extend the hedge and force the defense to switch. If you pick up your dribble when you see the flat hedge or soft show, you bail out the defense, as your defender recovers easily and there is no separation between the screener and his defender.

Defense Switches

If the defense switches, attack a mismatch (Figure 16). Posts screen for guards to prevent easy switches; if a guard screens for a guard, a switch does not create a mismatch. However, if the defense switches on a big-little screen, the post has a small defender and the guard has a slower defender. Exploit a mismatch. Do not rush.

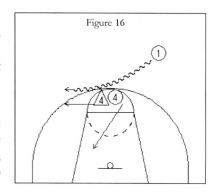

Figure 16

The post defender guarding a ball handler in space is a bigger mismatch. Create space with a fan or pull-back dribble and attack. If the post defender sags off to contain the dribble, shoot. If he tries to defend, make a quick move and get into the paint.

To get the ball to the post, wait for the screener to get to the block; do not make the screener catch a pass on the move and take a dribble against a smaller, quicker defender. Let the post get to the area where he has the advantage and get him the ball before the defense rotates.

Defense Traps

If the defender hedges high or traps, split the defenders (Figure 17) or use a pull-back dribble to create space (Figure 18). To split the defenders, create a little separation and then explode through the crease with a long, low dribble. To get the separation, use a slight hesitation dribble or fake a move to the outside of the hedger before pushing the ball between the defenders with a long dribble.

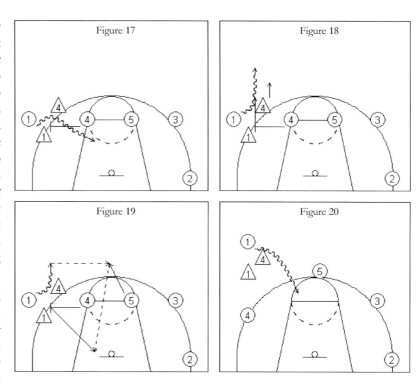

The pull-back dribble is a protect dribble: turn your inside shoulder toward the defender and use the width of your body to protect the ball while shuffling away. The worst move in a trap or hard hedge is to turn your back to the defense or pick up your dribble. Use the pull-back dribble to create a passing angle or space to attack.

As you move away from the defenders, the defenders trap aggressively or recover to their own man. If the defenders trap, the space creates a pass out of the trap (Figure 19) or a lane to attack: as the defender's close the distance, split a loose trap or attack one defender's outside shoulder (Figure 20). Beating one defender creates an offensive advantage.

Slip the Screen

If the defense shows the hedge or trap too early, the screener can slip the screen (Figure 21). As he runs to set the screen, if he feels his defender move out of position and give away the lane to the basket, he cuts to the basket rather than setting the screen.

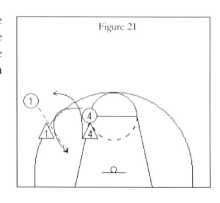

Figure 21

Review

- Attack aggressively
- Big screens for small
- Use two dribbles
- Be patient to exploit the mismatch against a switch

Games

Use *2v2 Games* to introduce the pick and roll and progress to 3v3 and 4v4 games which emphasize the pick and roll, like *4v4 On-Ball Cut Throat* and *3v3 Horns*.

Game: 2v2 Half-Court	
Objective	To give players space to run pick and rolls to learn to react to the defense and make the appropriate play.
Pre-Requisites	Protect dribble; fan dribble; crossover; lay-ups; passing off the dribble; hook pass; setting a screen.
Execution	Play 2v2 games to five baskets. On all changes of possession, offense clears beyond the three-point line with a pass. If the offense scores, they stay on offense. Start all dead ball situations with a check. Once the defense passes to the offense, the ball is live.
Progression I	If the defense switches all the screens, institute a rule where the defense cannot play an on-ball screen in the same way on consecutive screens. Another option is to eliminate all switches – but give the defense two exceptions. This requires more mature players: in the entire game, the defense can only switch the on-ball screen twice. Otherwise, they have to hedge, trap or just fight through, under or over the screen.
Teaching Points	Use the pick-and-roll; read the defense; show patience on a switch; roll to an open space; attack the hedger; be aggressive and look to turn the corner.

Game: 4v4 On-Ball Cut Throat	
Objective	To use different options of the pick-and-roll and adjust to help defenders.
Pre-Requisites	Protect dribble; fan dribble; crossover; lay-ups; passing off the dribble; hook pass; setting a screen.
Execution	Play *4v4 Cut Throat* with the stipulation that the offense cannot score until it runs at least one on-ball screen. Cut Throat involves multiple teams. If the offense scores, they stay on offense. New team sprints on the court as the defense. Old defense

	leaves the court and goes to the end of the line. If defense gets a rebound or a steal, they move to offense, and the offense goes to the end of the line. All out of bounds are rewarded to the defensive team. On any change of possession, the new offensive team must pass to the coach to check the ball. When the coach passes the ball to an offensive player, the ball is live.
Teaching Points	Spread the floor; communicate verbally or nonverbally when setting the screen; attack off the screen; read the help defenders – find the open player; use a hockey assist – the pass does not always have to go straight to the roller when he is open, sometimes the better play is to pass to a teammate with a better angle to the roller.

Game: 3v3 Horns

Objective	To work on using an on-ball screen, utilizing both players in the action and creating a more realistic defensive situation for the ball handler to read.
Pre-Requisite	Protect dribble; fan dribble; crossover; lay-ups; passing off the dribble; hook pass; setting a screen.
Execution	The "Horns" set is a very popular set where the two post players start above the elbows and set an on-ball screen for the guard who can choose to use either of the screens. 3v3 eliminates the wings and focuses the play on the actual screen and the interior play. Start with the ball handler near half court and the other two offensive players above the elbow. The ball handler uses the screen and the play is live. If offense scores, they stay on offense; if defense gets a rebound or steal, they outlet to the coach and move to offense. New team enters on defense.
Teaching Points	Communicate; switch the action of the posts – the screener can roll or pop and the other post pops or dives to the rim; read the defender; attack quickly; look to turn the corner.

Practice

After watching the games, determine the players' weaknesses or mistakes:

- Does the ball handler set up the screen properly?
- Does the screener set a good screen?
- Does the ball handler read the defense and make the right play?
- Does the ball handler's technical skill (ball handling, passing, shooting) break down?
- Is there good spacing?
- Does the ball handler allow the ball pressure to force a bad pass?

After determining the weakness, give the players feedback to assist with the learning. Drills without defense serve little purpose when teaching the pick-and-roll, unless the ball handler needs to practice the shots that he gets off the action, like shooting a pull-up jumper or shooting a three-pointer off a fan dribble.

Otherwise, use the same games to give the players more experience. If the ball handler struggles to read the initial defense, play more *2v2 Games* and force the defense to switch the way they defend the screen on each possession. 2v2 simplifies the reads because the ball handler is unconcerned with the help defenders and focuses all his attention on making the right play at the point of attack and then finishing the play. Also, to simplify the decision making for the point guard, use the *1v1 On-Ball Screen Drill*.

If the ball handler struggles with the decision-making after using the screen appropriately, use the same games to give the players more experience playing against help defenders in the on-ball situation. Work on spacing and movement away from the ball so the ball handler has easier passes and can make quicker decisions.

If the spacing breaks down, review the *String Spacing* concepts and their relation to the on-ball screen situations. The same options apply. The key is to make the players away from the ball more aware, so they make the on-ball screen more effective rather than congesting the court or standing and watching.

Drill: 1v1 On-Ball Screen

Objective	To read the defense properly and make the appropriate decision when using an on-ball screen.
Pre-Requisites	Protect dribble; fan dribble; crossover; lay-ups; shots off the dribble.
Drill Execution	Set up a chair as the screen and use a defender. As the ball handler reaches the screen, the defender chooses how to play the screen: hedge, trap or no help. The ball handler reads the defense and makes the appropriate play: if the defense hedges, extend the hedge; if he traps, use a pull-back dribble; if he does nothing, turn the corner, square shoulders to the rim and attack. If the ball handler makes the right decision, he attacks off his move and works on different shots.
Progression I	Set up a chair as the screen and use a defender on the screen. Play 1v1, but the ball handler must use the screen and the second defender plays until the ball handler beats the help. If the second defender traps, the two defenders play until the ball handler beats the trap and then it returns to 1v1; if the second defender hedges, he leaves when the on-ball defender recovers. If the offense scores, he stays on offense; if the defense gets a rebound or steal, he moves to offense and the new player enters on defense.
Teaching Points	Get low when using the screen; make a decision and be aggressive; create separation from the defenders to square shoulders to the basket.

To incorporate the pick-and-roll into technical drills, use the *Two-Ball Pick-and-Roll Series*:

Drill: Two-Ball Pick-and-Roll Series

Objective	To practice shots off a high on-ball screen action.
Pre-Requisites	Speed dribble; shots off the dribble; fan dribble.
Drill Execution	First line (L1) starts 35-feet from the basket; second line (L2) starts at the block;

	and third line (L3) starts in the baseline corner with a ball. L2 sprints to set a high on-ball screen; L1 attacks the screen and uses one of these options: (1) Hit a pull-up jumper at the elbow; (2) fan dribble, hesitate and attack for a pull-up jumper; (3) fan dribble wide, crossover and attack the key for a pull-up jumper; (4) fan dribble, hesitate and shoot the three. After L1 uses the screen, L2 rolls to the basket. L3 passes to L2 rolling to the basket. L3 rebounds L1's shot and goes to the end of L1; L1 goes to the end of L2; and L2 rebounds his shot and goes to the end of L3.
Teaching Points	Imagine a defender as you make the moves; game speed; balance on your shot.

Drill: Two-Ball Side Pick-and-Roll Series

Objective	To practice shots off a side on-ball screen.
Pre-Requisite	Speed dribble; shots off the dribble; fan dribble; crossover dribble.
Drill Execution	First line (L1) starts on the wing, the second line (L2) starts at the block and the third line (L3) starts on the opposite elbow with a ball. L2 sprints to set a side on-ball screen; L1 attacks the screen and uses one of these options: (1) Shoots an elbow jumper; (2) fan dribbles, hesitates and attacks for a pull-up jumper; (3) fan dribbles middle, crosses over and attacks the key; (4) fan dribbles, hesitates and shoots the three. After L1 uses the screen, L2 rolls to the basket and L3 passes to L2. L3 rebounds L1's shot and goes to the end of L1; L1 goes to the end of L2; and L2 rebounds his shot and goes to the end of L3.
Teaching Points	Imagine a defender as you make the moves; game speed; balance on your shot.

Most offensive plays involve three players in the immediate action: a passer, a screener and a cutter. The two-man skills are some exceptions, but even skills like the pick-and-roll or dribble-hand-off often include a third player, especially when the ball handler is trapped or the defense hedges hard on the screen, and the ball handler passes to a third player to make the pass to the screener rolling to the basket.

Three-man action on the strong side of the court gives an offensive team ideal spacing and allows the team to flow easily from a three-man play to the two-man game by reversing the ball to a player on the weak side, or to cut one player across the court as the ball reverses to create another three-man play.

The most basic three-man action is a screen; however, there are several different types of screens and locations. The basic options are the same, but their usage differs slightly. Some different screen options are a down screen, flare screen, back screen and cross screen.

SETTING A SCREEN

Setting a screen seems like a simple skill, yet many teams set ineffective and illegal screens. To set a good screen, the screener:

- Headhunts: the screener must find the defender and move to him rather than relying on the offensive player to run the defender into the screen.
- Jump stops a half step before running into the defender.
- Sets a strong screen with a wide base.
- Communicates verbally ("Use me!) or non-verbally (closed fist) with his teammate so the teammate knows that he is setting a screen for him.
- Moves opposite the cutter – if the cutter cuts to the basket, the screener rolls high; if the cutter cuts high, the screener rolls to the basket.

USING A SCREEN

Screening relies on the teamwork between the screener, cutter and passer. To use a screen, the cutter:

- Runs shoulder to shoulder off the screen to prevent his defender from fighting through the screen.
- Waits for the screen to be set to prevent a moving screen and to force the defender to show how he is going to defend the screen. St. Louis University Head Coach Rick Majerus says that it is better to be late than early when using a screen.
- Reads the defense and makes the appropriate cut.
- Shows a target to the passer.

The passer must be ready to pass to the cutter or the screener as soon as one is open. If the passer waits until the cutter is to the designated spot, for instance the three-point line, before he passes, the pass is too late, and the defender will have an angle to the ball. The passer needs to read the cut, see the open man and pass immediately leading his teammate in the direction of his cut.

DOWN SCREEN

The most common screen is a down screen. Many youth offenses start with the posts down screening for the guards to receive a pass to initiate the offense. Often, players run from spot to spot regardless of the defense, as the coach

Defense	Offense
Beats offensive player to the screen	Cuts Backdoor
Follows the offensive player around the screen	Curls off the screen toward ball and basket
Goes underneath the screen	Flares or fades away from the screen
Fights through the screen	Straight cuts away from the defense

stresses the importance of getting open on the wing when the team practices its offense 5v0. However, to use a screen effectively, the offense must read the defense and cut accordingly. The defense has five general ways to defend the screen:

1. Trail the offensive player (Figure 1)
2. Go under the screen (Figure 2)
3. Fight through the screen (Figure 3)
4. Slide over top of the screen: beat the offensive player to the screen (Figure 4)
5. Switch (Figure 5)

The general rule offensively is to create as much distance from the defender as possible. The offense must read the defense and make the appropriate cut. If the offensive player runs to the same spot, without recognizing the defense, the defense has an advantage. The defense, knowing where the offensive player plans to cut, can cheat, anticipate the screen and cut, and beat the offensive player to the designated spot. If the screener and cutter move to the same spot every time, it makes switching the screen easy. In a high school game last

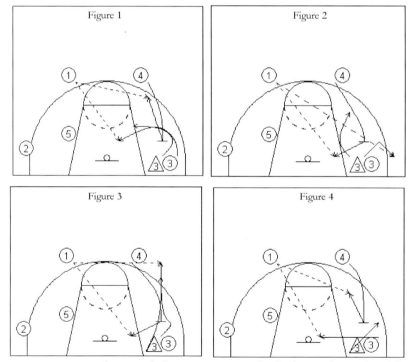

summer, a cutter ran to the same spot every time, and the passer never looked anywhere else. The team was committed to passing the ball from the point to the wing. After two possessions, the defense caught on, and the cutter's defender started to cheat. After four possessions, the cutter's defender and the screener's defender were racing each other to the wing to steal the pass. The passer never looked anywhere else; worse, the screener, who was wide open less than five feet from the rim, never looked for the ball. The down screen had only one option; consequently, the defense stole the point to wing pass on five straight possessions before the coach called timeout and switched to a new play, rather than passing to the screener for wide open lay-ups.

After setting the screen, the screener must roll to the basket or open to the ball. As with an on-ball screen, the screener can slip the screen if his defender moves to switch or hedge too early – if the defender gives him a clear lane to the basket, slip to the rim for the direct pass.

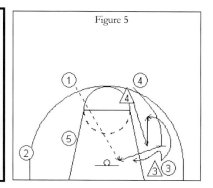
Figure 5

Questions to Resolve
1. How is my defender playing me?
2. What space is open for the cut?
3. How is the screener's defender playing the screen?
4. What are my strengths? Am I a shooter?
5. Am I cutting to get myself open or is my cut to free another player, like the screener?

Any time the defense switches, the screener is the primary target. Otherwise, the screener cuts opposite of the cutter and anticipates a pass. If a screener sets a great screen, he frees himself because his defender must help or switch. Passers must have a broad-external attention so they see the screener and the cutter – and their defenders – rather than focusing

Questions to Resolve (Screener)
1. How is my defender playing me?
2. Which way should I roll?
3. Do I pick and pop or screen and roll?
4. What is my strength: shooting or slashing to the basket?

only on the anticipated pass receiver. Former NBA Head Coach Hubie Brown says that you throw the pass away from the defense, rather than to the offense. Ideally, the passer reads the defense, anticipates the cut and leads the cutter with the pass as soon as he breaks away from the screener. Anticipating the pass sometimes leads to a mistake, as the passer sees one thing, but the cutter does another. When learning, instruct the players to call out their cut so the passer anticipates correctly (lead cueing), and the cutter thinks about the cut (long term memory retention). Encourage players to anticipate, so they react automatically without thinking.

Games

Use *3v3* and *4v4 Cut Throat* with an emphasis on screens; *3v3 Quarter Court* games and the *2v2 Utah Rules* to train setting and using screens.

Game: 2v2 Utah Rules	
Objective	To set good screens and to read the defense correctly, leading to immediate, open shots.
Pre-Requisites	Catch-and-shoot shots; v-cuts; chest pass; shooting footwork
Execution	P1 starts at the guard spot on offense defended by D1, and P2 starts on the wing defended by D2. Designated passer (DP) starts at the opposite guard spot. P1 passes to the DP and cuts to set a screen for P2. P2 v-cuts. If D1 cheats high to help on the screen or turns his back to P1, P1 cuts to the basket. Otherwise, P1 sets the screen for P2 and P2 uses the screen appropriately. Once DP enters the ball, the offense has one pass to score.

	P2 or P1 can catch and shoot or catch and drive. If the offense gets an offensive rebound, the ball is live. Possession ends when defense secures the ball or the offense scores. If offense scores, they stay on offense; new team enters on defense; defense must get a stop to play offense.
Teaching Points	Shoulder to shoulder; see the defense; show a target to the passer; cut hard; physical screens – embrace contact; roll hard; want the ball.

Game: 4v4 Cut Throat

Objective	To practice give-and-go cuts and squaring to the basket.
Pre-Requisite	Pivot foot; chest pass; bounce pass; V-cut; lay-ups.
Drill Execution	Cut Throat games involve multiple teams, at least three per basket. If offense scores, they stay on offense. New team sprints on the court as the defense. Old defense leaves the court and goes to the end of the line. If defense gets a rebound or a steal, they move to offense, and the offense goes to the end of the line. All out of bounds are rewarded to the defensive team. On any change of possession, the new offensive team must pass to the coach to check the ball. When the coach passes the ball to an offensive player, the ball is live.
Progression I	On any reception, player must square to the basket, or it is a turnover. On any pass, the passer must cut to the basket; otherwise, it is a turnover.
Progression II	Count baskets scored directly from a screen away from the ball.
Progression IV	No dribbling.
Teaching Points	Square quickly to the basket; cut hard; cut and replace; read the defense; set screens; be physical; communicate; stay active – no standing.

Game: 3v3 Quarter Court

Objective	To train hard, aggressive cuts and passing under pressure.
Pre-Requisites	Pivot foot; V-cuts; bounce pass; chest pass; wrap-around pass; lay-ups.
Drill Execution	Divide the team into three-person teams. Divide the half-court in half; the action stays on one side of the court. After a pass, the passer screens for the other teammate or receives a screen. Pass and screen until the offense creates a good shot. The offense can dribble, but no on-ball screens allowed. If offense scores, they stay on offense. New team sprints on the court as the defense. Old defense leaves the court and goes to the end of the line. If defense gets a rebound or a steal, they move to offense, and the offense goes to the end of the line. All out of bounds are rewarded to the defensive team. On any change of possession, the new offensive team must pass to the coach to check the ball. When the coach passes the ball to an offensive player, the ball is live.
Teaching Points	Set up the cut; cut and replace; keep moving; be strong with the ball; be ready to make the pass; set strong screens; read your teammate's cut and anticipate the correct pass; don't forget the screener; be creative with screens and cuts.

Practice

When a mistake occurs, determine the real root of the mistake:

- Did the cutter make the wrong cut?
- Did the cutter cut too early?
- Did the passer make the wrong pass?
- Did the passer pass too late?
- Did the passer not see the help defender or the switch?
- Did the screener set a weak screen?

When turnovers happen, it is rarely the technical execution. Mistakes occur because of poor decision-making skills, so focus instruction and questions on the decisions, not the actual pass or mistake. Everyone sees the ball rolling out of bounds. Obviously, someone made a mistake. But, what was the mistake? Was it a poorly executed pass or the wrong pass? Why?

For most errors, simplify the game by reducing the number of players or eliminating the dribble. If problems persist, especially with the cutter making the wrong cuts, use the *Utes' Shooting Drill* to slowly develop the skill and to practice shooting off different cuts.

Drill: **Utes Shooting**	
Objective	To work on game shooting off different cuts.
Pre-Requisites	Shooting footwork; catch-and-shoot shots.
Drill Execution	Set up a chair (screener) where the offense typically sets the down screen within the team's system. Form a line on the wing (L1) and another line on the opposite side at the guard spot (L2). L1 cuts, uses the imaginary screen, catches and shoots. The player calls out the cut as he makes it: Flare, Tight Curl, Loose Curl or Backdoor. L1 follows his shot, rebounds and goes to the end of L2, while L2 follows his pass to the end of L1.
Progression I	Use a form defender so the cutter must read the defender, make the correct cut, catch and shoot. The defender picks one way to defend the cutter (goes underneath, trails, fights through), and the cutter must make the right cut.
Teaching Points	Footwork on the catch; communicate; get balanced before the shot; use an inside pivot foot; anticipate the shot as you cut to the ball; show a target.

CROSS SCREENS

Cross screens are the second basic type of screen away from the ball, and often the first screen introduced to youth players through underneath out of bounds plays or press breaks. The cross screen works like the down screen with slight adjustments for the spacing and defense.

Rather than the screener moving from high to low to set the screen, the screener moves across the court. For an underneath out of bounds play, the screener cuts from the left block to the right block to set the screen (Figure 6).

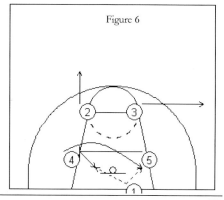

Figure 6

Because of the proximity to the basket on an underneath out of bounds play, most teams fight through the screen or switch. However, on general cross screens, the defense uses the same five options as with the down screen, and the offensive player makes the same basic cuts.

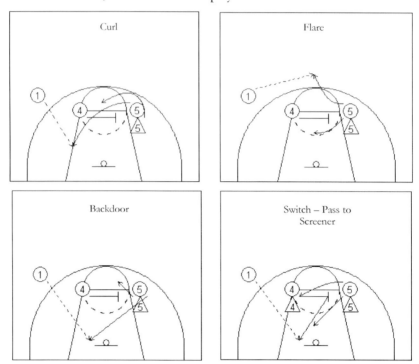

On cross screens, especially those near the basket, the defense often switches, so cross screens are the best screens away from the ball to use to teach the roll or seal after a screen. If a player sets a great screen, he increases the likelihood of a switch; if he knows how to seal after the switch, he can create a passing angle and establish good position close to the basket. When players set great screens and use their bodies to establish position, they improve the effectiveness of the underneath out of bounds plays.

Besides out of bounds plays, cross screens are a staple of motion offenses, especially those which use two low post players. A Flex screen is a type of cross screen as well. In an offense with two low post players, one often screens across for the other to help the player establish deep post position. On Flex screens, the cutter runs into the screen, rather than the screener head-hunting, but the screening action is similar. In most Flex offenses, the screener receives a down screen after the Flex screen; however, some teams use the screener to roll back to the ball, giving the passer two options off the screen, especially if the team switches the Flex screen to eliminate the first cutter.

Games

Use *3v3* and *4v4 Cut Throat* to practice cross screens. Another game is *2v2 Post Play*. While most coaches teach guard skills to all players, few coaches or programs really teach post-specific skills to any players. Every player, regardless of size or position, benefits from post skill development.

Game: 2v2 Post Play

Objective	To establish post position, create a passing lane and make post moves.
Pre-Requisites	Post moves; bounce passes; wrap-around pass; pivot foot; shot fake; power lay-ups; baby hooks.
Execution	One player/coach starts on the wing as a passer with the ball. Two offensive players and two defenders start in the key. The offense maintains possession until the defense gets a rebound or steal; there are no out of bounds. The offensive players can pass out to the passer at any time and receive a return pass. The offensive players must stay within the "post" area: elbow, block, short corner, key. If a loose ball goes outside the area, whoever retrieves the ball passes to the passer and receives the ball once they return to the live area. A made basket is a live ball: whoever rebounds the ball out of the net outlets to the passer and is on offense. Passer calls fouls: a foul on the shot is a basket. Play to three baskets.
Teaching Points	Use your body; work together; set screens and seal; attack the basket; maintain spacing within the confined area; balance; call for the ball with your body language and voice; keep the defender's hands out of the passing lane.

Game: 4v4 Box Cut Throat

Objective	To set physical screens, pass in tight spaces and finish contested shots.
Pre-Requisites	Post moves; bounce passes; wrap-around pass; pivot foot; shot fake; power lay-ups; baby hooks; shooting footwork.
Execution	Play 4v4 Cut Throat in a box formation: offensive players set cross screens and down screens, but must stay within a confined box (three feet wider than the key) except when a defender goes under a down screen and the offensive player flares to the corner. On the flare, if he does not catch and shoot, he fills the vacated spot in the box as soon as he passes to a teammate. On a pass to the low post, the passer can basket cut or cross screen; if he cuts, the other players cut to fill the openings in the box (*Cut & Replace*). Play until the offense scores or the defense secures the ball. The winner plays offense and new team enters on defense; loser goes to the end of the line.
Teaching Points	Be physical; show a target; read the defense; be creative with screens; gather before shooting; use pass and ball fakes when necessary; cut aggressively; get the defender's hands out of the passing lane.

Practice

After observing the players, determine the cause of the mistakes:

- Do the players read the defense or run to spots?
- Does the passer stare at the cutter leading to tipped passes?
- Does the screener role into an open space?
- Do the players work together to create an advantage?
- Does the pass receiver receive the ball on balance and make a strong move?

Cutters need to use the screen rather than running to a pre-ordained spot. Punish the defense, regardless of how they defend the screen. The passer must prepare to pass to the open player and use fakes and his eyes to create a passing lane to the open player when he first gets open, not after he stops moving. If the problem is the pass reception or the finish, use a build-up lay-up drill to train the catch and finish when cutting past the rim. Otherwise, continue with the small-sided games and add more feedback to cue the players to the proper cuts, reads and passes.

Drill: Flex Lay-ups

Objective	To catch, gather and make lay-ups when moving away from the basket.
Pre-Requisite	Power lay-ups; baby hooks; front pivot; reverse pivot; V-cuts.
Execution	Form one line in the right baseline corner (L1) with a player on the right block (L2) and a second line at the left elbow (L3) with the balls. L1 uses L2 as a screen and cuts toward the left block. L2 follows L1 as a half-speed defender. L3 passes to L1 once he clears the screen. L1 catches and finishes. L2 plays soft defense, applying pressure to the shot, but not trying to block the shot. L1 shoots and then replaces L2 as the next screener. L2 gets the rebound and takes the ball to the end of L3. The passer sprints to the back of L1.
Teaching Points	Gather on the catch – regain balance before shooting; use a reverse lay-up or a stride stop to finish; show a target; protect the ball; use pump fakes and pivots if necessary; be physical with the defender.

POST SPLITS

Another three-man action which involves basic skills is the post split. This action uses basket cuts, down screens, dribble hand-offs and more. The Triangle offense uses the post split in the mid-post area and Rick Adelman's Kings used this concept from the high post. The action initiates with three players on the strong side and a pass from the wing to the post (Figure 7). From there, the options are limitless, as the correct spacing and a couple basic tactical skills (give-and-go, down screen, dribble hand-off) create plenty of options for the offense if it reads the defense correctly.

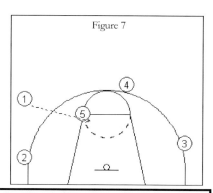

Figure 7

The passer's (P1) first option is a give-and-go to the basket (Figure 8). He passes to P5 and cuts to the rim. The baseline player (P2) fills the vacated spot left by the cutter. If P2's defender helps on the cut to the basket, he will be a step behind P2, leaving P2 open for a three-point shot or to curl

Questions for the Passer to Resolve
1. Which cut is open?
2. How are they defending my teammates?
3. Do I have a passing lane? How is my defender playing me?
4. Where are the weak side/help defenders?
5. After the pass, do I cut to the basket, set an on-ball screen or screen away?

around the post (P5) for a dribble hand-off (Figure 9).

After the pass to the post, P1 can set a down screen for P2. Reading the defense and setting up the screen create several options, especially when teammates get a feel for playing together. As with any down screen, one player cuts to the basket and one player cuts away from the basket.

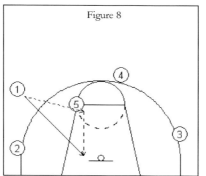

Figure 8

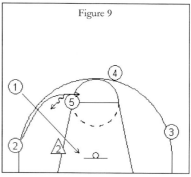

Figure 9

Players also read the defense and decide whether to cut back door, slip the screen, flare or curl.

On the pass, P1 cuts to set the screen and P2 cuts to set up the screen (Figure 10). Each player reads his defender and his teammate. If P1's defender starts to hedge or switch to prevent P2 from curling tight to the basket, P1 slips the screen to the basket (Figure 11). If P1 slips the screen, P2 cuts toward the post for a dribble-hand-off (Figure 12). If P2's defender beats P2 to the screen, P2 sets up the screen and cuts backdoor. If P2 cuts backdoor, P1 quickly flares to the three-point line (Figure 13).

There are many options involving the screen: P1 can set the screen and P2 can flare to the corner for a three-pointer while P1 dives to the rim; P2 can curl off the screen toward P5 and P1 can flare to the corner; P2 can curl toward P5 and then flare behind P5 for a three-pointer if his defender tries to race underneath the hand-off. Again, the possibilities are numerous and rely on the basic tactical skills discussed earlier coupled with reading the defense correctly.

Questions for the Cutters to Resolve

1. How is my defender playing me?
2. Is the basket cut open?
3. Is the passer ready to pass or will he initiate a dribble-at?
4. After the cut, if I do not get the ball, do I replace myself or empty to the weak side corner?
5. Where do I want the ball?
6. How do I set up my defender to create the play that I want?

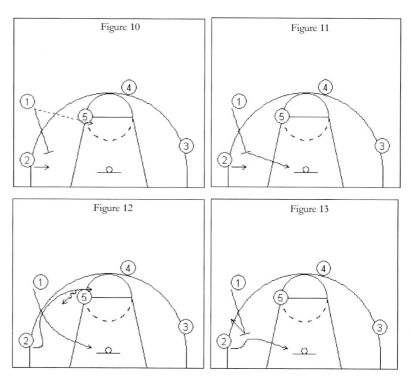

Figure 10

Figure 11

Figure 12

Figure 13

Games

To train these skills, play 3v3 on one side of the court and initiate the play with a pass to the high post or mid-post, whichever you prefer ^{Figure 12}; high post receives the ^{Figure 13} play is live, but players must stay on the strong side. If the initial action does not work or does not produce a shot, players learn to adapt to the situation. If one player cuts to the rim and is not open, and the other flares to the three-point, but does not have an open shot, the post can set an on-ball screen. At this point, players have experience using all the basic tactical skills; now, they need to read the situation and communicate with each other.

Game: 3v3 Quarter Court Post Splits	
Objective	To train reading the defense on cuts and screens.
Pre-Requisites	Pivot foot; V-cuts; bounce pass; chest pass; wrap-around pass; lay-ups.
Drill Execution	Divide the team into three-person teams. Divide the half-court in half; the action stays on one side of the court. Initiate the play with a pass into the high post. Cut and screen until the offense creates a good shot. The offense can dribble. If the offense scores, they stay on offense. New team sprints on the court as the defense. Old defense leaves the court and goes to the end of the line. If the defense gets a rebound or a steal, they move to offense, and the offense goes to the end of the line. All out of bounds are rewarded to the defensive team. On any change of possession, the new offensive team must pass to the coach to check the ball.
Teaching Points	Set up the cut; cut and replace; keep moving; be strong with the ball; be ready to make the pass; set strong screens; read your teammate's cut and anticipate the correct pass; don't forget the screener.

Practice

After observing the players in action, evaluate the mistakes:

- Are the players' technical skills (dribbling, shooting, passing) breaking down?
- Are the players' tactical skills (give-and-go, dribble-at, down screens) breaking down?
- Are the players' decision-making skills responsible for the mistakes?

If the mistakes occur because of technical skill break down, return to the early chapters to practice live ball moves, dribble moves, passing and getting open. Also, the break down drills for the different tactical skills, like the *Utes' Shooting Drill*, *Two-Ball Pick-and-Roll Series* and *Dribble-at Lay-up Series* offer technical skill practice specific to the different tactical skills.

If the tactical skills break down, return to the specific section and use the games for the particular tactical skill. If the decision-making breaks down, continue with the *3v3 Quarter Court Posts Splits* or return to one of the games using the skill which breaks down. If the players are not reading the down screen, play more *2v2 Utah Rules* to practice using general down screens and then return to *3v3 Quarter Court Posts Splits* to train the specific screens in the post splits.

HIGH-LOW

The High-Low is another concept that depends on spacing and technical skills like post footwork and passing. When a team takes away a pass from the wing into the post, the high-low pass is available. On a ball reversal to the top, the low post reverse pivots on his top foot to seal the defender and create a passing lane to the basket.

One entry into a high-low is through a high on-ball screen. In a Horns' set, the point guard dribbles off a high screen to either side. The screener rolls to the basket with the other post filling high (Figure 14), or the other post dives to the rim while the screener pops high (Figure 15). On the reversal to the top, the low post seals in the lane for the high-low entry pass.

When the post rolls to the basket, the defense (cone) often plays on the high side (Photo 1), which is why the ball handler is unable to pass the ball directly to the post (Figure 16).

On the reversal to the top, the post holds his position and pivots with his top foot. As he pivots, he calls for the ball with his outside hand looking for the lob pass over his defender (Photo 2). If the defense plays below the post player as he rolls to the basket, he uses a "Don Nelson Move" to seal the defender: he walks into the defender and puts one foot between the defender's legs. As the pass reverses to the top, he reverse pivots on this foot and sits on the defender's leg, sealing the defender and creating a clear passing lane for the man at the top.

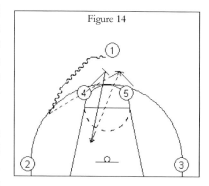

Figure 14

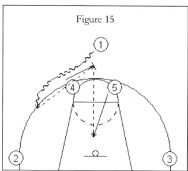

Questions to Resolve
1. On what side is the defense?
2. Where is the passing angle? Direct pass or lob pass?
3. Where is the help defense? Is the passing lane *really* open?
4. Can the post player effectively hold his position?

Photo 1   Photo 2

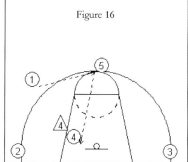

Figure 15

Figure 16

Games

Use the *2v2 Post Play* and *3v3 Horns* games to train the High-Low action. Play *3v3 Horns* with two post players per team and rotate the guards at the top.

Game: 3v3 Horns

Objective	To work on using an on-ball screen and creating a high-low action.
Pre-Requisite	Protect dribble; fan dribble; crossover; lay-ups; passing off the dribble; hook pass; setting a screen.
Execution	The "Horns" set is a very popular set where the two post players start above the elbows and set an on-ball screen for the guard who can choose to use either of the screens. 3v3 eliminates the wings and focuses the play on the actual screen and the interior play. Start with the ball handler at half court and the other two offensive players above the elbow. The ball handler uses the screen and the play is live. If offense scores, they stay on offense; if defense gets a rebound or steal, they outlet to the coach and move to offense. New team enters on defense.
Teaching Points	Communicate; switch the action of the posts – the screener can roll or pop and the other post pops or dives to the rim; read the defender; attack quickly.

Practice

After observing the game action, determine the mistake. With the High-Low, the most common mistake is the post footwork when trying to hold position as the ball rotates from the wing to the top. Use a break down drill to teach the footwork against a form defender and then quickly return to the action. Making a reverse pivot is rarely the problem; the problem occurs when the defender is present and the player must make the pivot and hold position to call for the pass.

When the post player seals for the lob, he should:

- Keep both hands high. If you put a forearm in the defender to hold position, officials tend to call push-offs on the pass.
- Wait until the ball is overhead to move. If you move too early, and release contact, the defender has an equal chance to steal the ball. Wait until you see the ball overhead between your hands to go and grab the ball.
- Use your hip and lower body to create contact with the defender and hold your position.
- Pivot to the basket on the catch and square shoulders to the backboard.

If mistakes persist, decide the cause of the errors:

- Is the pass too high or too low?
- Does the low post create contact on his pivot to hold his position?
- Does he release his seal too soon creating a 50/50 ball?
- Is the passer's defender forcing a bad pass?
- Does the passer have a lane to drive rather than throwing the lob pass?

If the problem is the technical skill of the passer, return to Chapter 3 and work on passing technique. On a lob pass, the passer should aim just short of the bottom corner of the backboard. If the post player continues to struggle with his footwork, use the break down session or continue with the games, offering more feedback. Post players tend to develop more slowly than guards because they rarely get meaningful practice against live defenders, so they may need more time to practice their moves and footwork against an actual defensive player before they feel confident. If the players need more experience, use the *2v2 Post Play* game, but turn it into a drill where players rotate against live defense, but it is less competitive, and build back to the live game. The goal is to develop confident players and to learn new skills, and sometimes players do not try new things in competitive situations. Use the same set-up, but change the emphasis from competition to training or teaching so players focus more on learning the proper footwork, and less on winning the game.

As players understand the basic tactical skills and develop a base level of basketball intelligence, they can transition to the 5v5 game and play a true motion offense without the coach turning "motion" into a structured play. Depending on personnel, a coach might teach some, but not all of the tactical skills or emphasize certain skills through his principles. For instance, a team lacking a strong point guard might emphasize more cuts and off-ball screens and fewer on-ball screens, while a team full of penetrating guards might emphasize spacing, McKay's six sections and on-ball screens.

In essence, however, once players understand the different elements, five-man offense simply combines different parts into a complete offense like words combing together to form a sentence. In the first example (Figure1), the team uses a high on-ball screen; however, the action depends on the team understanding court spacing and using the *string spacing* concepts.

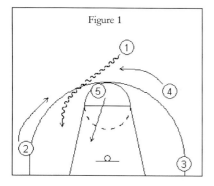

Figure 1

As P1 uses the on-ball screen, P5 rolls to the open area. Since P5 rolls to the rim, P2 has two options: spot up in the corner or loop behind the dribble. As P1 dribbles into P2's area, he loops to vacate the area. P4 starts one pass away from P1, so he follows P1 as P1 dribbles away from him. P3, two passes away on the weak side, remains in the corner for the baseline pass.

The players' movement makes P1's decision-making easier. He anticipates the movement because the team shares a set of principles, so he knows, for instance, that P4 is open rotating to the top of the key even if he does not see him.

As P1 uses the on-ball screen, he decides whether to attack the rim. If D5 hedges and allows D1 to recover, P1 may not have a lane to the basket. If P1 beats the hedge, D2 could help on the ball and prevent the lay-up, leading to a back door for P2 or a kick for a three-pointer.

If P1 decides against attacking the rim, he searches for his best option. If D5 hedges, P5 probably has some advantage either on the roll or once he posts up on the block. P1 could make a quick pass to P2 in the corner who could feed P5. Or, as P2 clears out, P1 could keep his dribble alive and feed P5 in the post.

If P5 is not open on the block, D5 might have help from D3. If D3 helps on the strong side block, a skip pass to the corner gets P3 a wide open three-pointer. Or, if D4 helps the helper and drops to eliminate the skip pass to the corner, P4 is wide open at the top of the key. Because of the spacing, it is almost impossible for the defense to eliminate all the options. The spacing and the simple maneuver disorganizes the defense, so the defense has to prioritize or gamble.

If the defense gambles and traps the on-ball screen (Figure 2), the players use their basic spacing principles for any trap: *Diamond Spacing.* P4 rotates behind the dribble, cutting slightly higher than before to give P1 a better passing angle as he uses his retreat dribble to create space. P5 opens to the middle, posting up in the center of the court if P1 is able to split D1 and D5 with the pass. P2 sprints up the sideline to shorten the distance of a pass to P2. The defense cannot trap the ball, protect the basket and deny all three passes. If D3 rotates up to deny D5, P3 is wide open at the front of the rim for a long pass

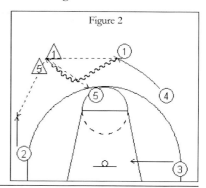

Figure 2

or a "hockey assist" through P2, P5 or P4. If P1 manages to pass to P2 or P5, it creates a 2v1 advantage with P3 against D3. Even if the ball rotates back to P4, a quick pass to P3 cutting to the wing opens the lane for P5 to cut to the rim unguarded.

The play depends on the defense's choices, but the offense's spacing and principles create the offensive advantage, even as the defense applies more pressure and gambles for the steal. A team which lacks principles or which has a sophisticated press break may take too much time to adjust to the trap or may lack the spacing required to create an offensive advantage out of the defensive pressure. Rather than thinking about the exact spot to cut to in a press break or to attack a half-court trap, the players know exactly how to react to a trap and they find the appropriate open space. The difference between an automatic reaction and a player thinking about different options is a second or more, which is the difference between a lay-up off a steal for the defense and a lay-up off two quick passes for the offense.

These are two examples of how different basic skills combine together for an offensive attack. Another example of an offense using basic skills is a play combining frequent concepts from the Detroit Pistons and Phoenix Suns.

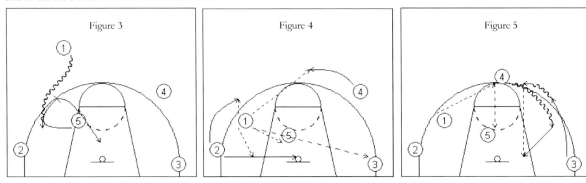

The play starts with an on-ball screen set by P5 who rolls to the rim (Figure 3). P1 uses the screen and tries to turn the corner toward the rim. Because of the angle of the screen, P1 attacks "down hill" with shoulders squared to the basket, which puts even more pressure on the defense to hedge or switch. P3 holds his position in the opposite corner in case P1 or P5 get stuck along the baseline with the ball. P2 and P4 move based on the *String Spacing* principles. P2 can cut backdoor immediately or he can loop behind the ball. P4 follows the dribble penetration. P1 has four passing options: ideally, P5 is open rolling down the lane for a lay-up; if not, P3, P4 and P2 space around the three-point line waiting for a catch-and-shoot jump shot (Figure 4).

If the ball rotates to P4 at the top, and he is not open for a jump shot, he looks at P5 for the high-low pass. If that is unavailable, he dribbles the ball to the weak side to initiate a dribble-at with P3 (Figure 5). P3 can cut back door to the rim or loop behind for the dribble hand-off. The difference between P1's initial penetration and P4's penetration is the drive's angle and the players involved. A dribble-at involves a post player dribbling at a guard; when two guards are involved, P1 and P2, the dribble-at does not create an advantage on a switch. To run a dribble-at, the ball handler attacks directly toward the receiver's defender, while with P1's initial penetration, P1 attacks toward the basket.

As P3 penetrates off the hand-off, P2 spots up in the opposite corner, P1 spots up on the opposite wing and P4 rolls to the basket. This play is an example of a two-man action leading to a two-man action on the other side. On the ball reversal, no players cut with the ball: P2, P5 and P1 remain on one side and allow P4 and P3 the space to run the two-man game on the left side.

The simple play uses several basic concepts and gives the offense numerous different actions to create an easy shot. It forces the defense to play the width of the court and defend multiple situations. Regardless of the defense's decisions, the offense has a counter to exploit the defense. The offense reads the defense and makes the appropriate play.

An offensive attack can flow from a two-man play into a three-man play. For instance, the following uses an on-ball screen on one side followed by a post split as the three-man action. The offense initiates with a give-and-go cut by P1 (Figure 6) followed by P5 cutting to set the on-ball screen for P2. P1 receives a staggered screen, while P2 and P5 run the pick and roll (Figure 7). If P2 is unable to create a shot or pass to P5 rolling to the basket, he passes to P1. P1 swings the ball to P3 and sprints to the corner (Figure 8). P3 passes into P4 in the high post and sets the down screen for P1 (Figure 9). In this case, P1 curls tight off the screen to the basket and P3 flares to the three-point line.

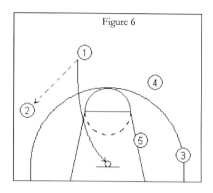

Figure 6

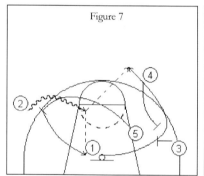

Figure 7

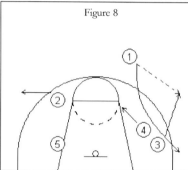

Figure 8

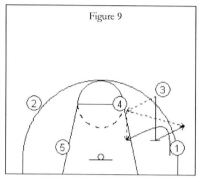

Figure 9

When the initial action leads into a three-man play, a cutter, in this case P1, cuts from one side to the other. The Flex offense is nothing but a series of three-man plays with a cross screen always followed by a down screen.

Effective offense incorporates these concepts in different ways and in different locations. The team's principles organize the attack, so each player anticipates the actions of his teammates. A ball handler anticipates his teammate's movement as he dribble penetrates, but teammates also anticipate the next action: in the last example, on the ball reversal the team looks for the post split. Other examples could be to run a pick and roll on a ball reversal or a dribble-at.

Teams can use all the different tactical skills or a coach can emphasize or choose only one or two skills to use over and over. A Princeton-style offense uses give-and-go cuts and dribble-ats over and over until it creates a backdoor lay-up or open three-point shot. Occasionally the high post might set a back screen, but the primary offense is give-and-go cuts with dribble-ats.

In Figure 10, P1 passes to P3 and uses a back screen from P5. In Figure 11, P3 dribbles at P2, while P1 fills behind the dribble. P2 cuts back door; if he is open, P3 passes to P2. If not, P3 passes to P4 and cuts off a back screen by P5 (Figure 12). P4 reverses to P5 and P1 cuts back door (Figure 13). P5 dribbles at P3 who cuts behind and shoots the three-pointer (Figure 14).

These are just a couple basic ideas. Once players learn the different general concepts and learn to read the defense and anticipate their teammates' movement, the offensive options are unlimited.

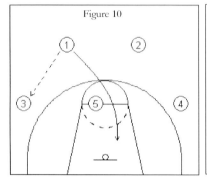

Figure 10

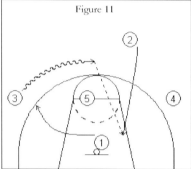

Figure 11

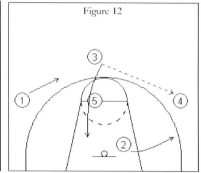

Figure 12

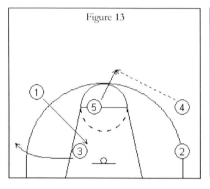

Figure 13

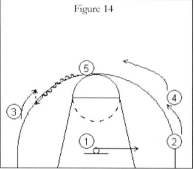

Figure 14

- Ericsson, K. Anders. (1996). The Road to Excellence. Mahwah, New Jersey: Lawrence Erlbaum Associates, Publishers.

- Farrey, Tom. "College Basketball – Like Father, Like Son." *The Seattle Times*, February 13, 1995.

- Griffin, Linda L. and Butler, Joy I. (2005). Teaching Games for Understanding. Champaign, IL: Human Kinetics.

- Kidman, Lynn. (2001). Developing Decision Makers. Christchurch, New Zealand: Innovative Print Communications Ltd.

- McCallum, Jack. "Charlotte's Web," *Sports Illustrated*: November 17, 2008.

- Nater, Swen and Gallimore, Ronald. You Haven't Taught until They Have Learned. Morgantown, West Virginia: Fitness Information Technology.

- Nideffer, Robert M. "Concentration Training for Peak Performance." Retrieved from http://www.peaksports.com/pdfs/concentration_training.pdf.

- Peppler, Mary Jo. (2002). "Using New and Proven Teaching Techniques," The Volleyball Coaching Bible. Champaign, IL: Human Kinetics.

- Peterson, Dan. "The Sports Cognition Framework," *Sports Are 80 Percent Mental*: April 10, 2008.

- Schmidt, Richard A. "Principles of Practice." *USOC Olympic Coach*, Fall 2008, Volume 20, Number 4.

- Schmidt, Richard A. and Bjork, Robert A. "New Conceptualizations of Practice: Common Principles in Three Paradigms Suggest New Concepts for Training." *Psychological Science*. Vol. 3, No. 4 July 1992.

- Vickers, Joan. Interview on PBS.org: "Science Hotline." Retrieved from www.pbs.org/saf/1206/hotline/hvickers.htm.

- Villepreux, Pierre. "Decision Making in Rugby." Retrieved from *www.rugbycoach.com/documents/DecisionMaking.pdf*.

- Ward, Paul and Williams, A. Mark. "Perceptual and cognitive skill development in soccer: the multidimensional nature of expert performance." *Journal of Sport and Exercise Psychology, 25*, 1, 93-111, 2003.

- Williams, Mark and North, Jamie. "Developing Anticipation in Sport." *Coaching Edge*. Issue 5, August 25, 2006.

- Williams, A. Mark; Ward, Paul; Knowles, John M.; and Smeeton, Nicholas J. "Anticipation Skill in a Real-World Task: Measurement, Training and Transfer in Tennis." *Journal of Experimental Psychology: Applied*. 2002, Vol. 8, No. 4, 259-270.

- Wein, Horst. (2004). Developing Game Intelligence in Soccer. Spring City, PA: Reedswain Publishing.

Brian McCormick is the Founder of **The Cross Over Movement**, a grassroots effort to improve youth basketball development based on <u>Cross Over: The New Model of Youth Basketball Development,</u> which he first published in 2006 and is now in its Third Edition.

McCormick is the Performance Director for trainforhoops.com and the Technical Director of 180Shooter.com. He writes a weekly newsletter received by coaches in over 35 countries and trains youth, college and professional players in Southern California and presents athlete and coach seminars for the Positive Coaching Alliance.

McCormick received his B.A. in American Literature and Culture from UCLA, where he directed the UCLA Special Olympics program and rowed for the UCLA Crew team, and a Master's in Sports Science from the United States Sports Academy.

He coached professionally in Sweden, where he was selected to coach in the All-Star Game, and Ireland. He has directed camps in Canada, China, Greece, Macedonia, Morocco, South Africa and Trinidad & Tobago and coached at the college, high school, CYO and AAU levels.

McCormick is a Certified Strength and Conditioning Specialist through the National Strength and Conditioning Association; Performance Enhancement Specialist through the National Academy of Sports Medicine; Sports Performance Coach through USA Weightlifting; and Level I Coach through USA Track and Field.

McCormick consults with youth basketball organizations and basketball facilities in the United States and abroad. For more information, visit **The Cross Over Movement** web site: thecrossovermovement.com. To subscribe to the free Hard2Guard Player Development Newsletter, email hard2guardinc@yahoo.com.

For more information, visit:

www.developyourbballiq.com

www.thecrossovermovement.com

www.180shooter.com

www.trainforhoops.com